FOREVER TARNISHED

FOREVER TARNISHED

JENNIFER GERKEN

Palmetto Publishing Group
Charleston, SC

Forever Tarnished
Copyright © 2020 by Jennifer Gerken
All rights reserved

No portion of this book may be reproduced, stored in a retrieval system, or transmitted in any form by any means–electronic, mechanical, photocopy, recording, or other except for brief quotations in printed reviews, without prior permission of the author.

First Edition

Printed in the United States

ISBN-13: 978-1-64111-813-2
ISBN-10: 1-64111-813-X

CONTENTS

Author's Note	ix
Chapter 1: Escape	1
Chapter 2: Unwanted Touches	13
Chapter 3: Abandonment	22
Chapter 4: Cheaters	33
Chapter 5: Trapped	46
Chapter 6: Loss	53
Chapter 7: Nana	62
Chapter 8: Noah	70
Chapter 9: Subpoena	78
Chapter 10: Empath	85
Chapter 11: Trial	92
Chapter 12: Fling	99
Chapter 13: Farewell	110
Chapter 14: Suicidal	113
Chapter 15: Addicts	117
Chapter 16: Emotional Neglect	122
Epilogue	125

To those who have struggled. You are not alone.

AUTHOR'S NOTE

I am writing this book in hopes of helping myself and others. I have had several life experiences that have brought me to where I am today, which is on the edge of a breakdown. My whole life, I have not dealt with things head-on. Instead, I buried them, telling myself, "I will be OK." But the truth is, I am almost forty now, and I've realized that I am *not* OK.

I have suffered from depression and anxiety off and on since I was sixteen years old. After the doctors tried me on prescription after prescription for about twenty years, like I was some sort of lab rat, I was referred to a psychiatrist. I never realized what a toll depression and anxiety can take on a person. These past two years have been by far the worst my depression and anxiety has ever been. It has taken both a physical and mental toll on me.

I spent an entire year driving to work daily, wishing I would find the courage to drive my car into the back end of a semi, or better yet, hoping I'd get in a car accident that would kill me. Not to mention I have recently started having panic attacks and developing all of these new habits, such as grinding my teeth, which kills my jaw and increases my migraines. If I drag my tongue along the bottom of my top front teeth, I can feel the unevenness from chiseling my teeth away; I've been unaware that I am even doing so. I also started this weird habit of pointing my toes toward the ceiling. Sounds silly, huh? Why don't you try it for a few minutes, because I guarantee you will feel the pressure on the top of your foot that it causes? Now, once you tried it+, imagine holding the position for hours. My feet feel like they have been run over by the end of the day. My body aches. I want to scream and cry. Some days, I do cry. Most days it is uncontrollable. I absolutely hate it, and I hate it even more that I have a family who thinks it's a joke. Or at least, that is how they make me feel when they make stupid comments like "Which Jen am I talking to today?" Depression is not a joke or a choice. I have struggled with this for decades. I have never felt so low or sick until now. I am not a suicidal person, and I'd never kill myself, so why am I daydreaming about this stuff when I know damn well I have plenty to be thankful for? I have two beautiful daughters to live for, and believe me, although being a single mom is tough at times, I'd never take my life. I live for these two girls. They are my world. So what is my problem? Why do I have these thoughts? Am I crazy, like everyone thinks? Or is this intense mental distress I've been dealing with finally taken over? It sure feels like I am not in control anymore.

In this book, I am going to discuss the many corrupted relationships I have had over the years with family, friends, and lovers. I am going to discuss secrets I kept buried and many other life events with which I did not deal well. My hope is that you learn to deal with your emotions and whatever life throws at you before it is too late and you end up in a nuthouse, or you develop these stress-related habits that take a toll on your body, or even worse…take your life. It is not good to keep things bottled up, my friends. Trust me.

AUTHOR'S NOTE

I am also hoping it helps you to become more self-aware in certain situations. To me, everything I dealt with seemed pretty normal. After all, I know others have it far worse than I have. Keeping secrets and not dealing with my emotions has come out in ways I didn't know were possible. I want everyone who reads this to understand what depression and anxiety is really like and the importance that not dealing with your emotions can have on you.

> Dear Self,
>
> I know it has been a long road of heartaches, pain, loss, depression, and anxiety. But just know that there is light at the end of the tunnel. You are stronger than you know and braver than you believe. You are a beautiful Woman who has not let hardships define her, and for that, you are an amazing human being. Please continue to stay strong for yourself and your girls. Remember to value yourself, love and respect yourself, and most importantly, stay true to yourself. Never doubt your worth and settle for nothing less than the <u>best</u>.
>
> Love always,
> Yourself

CHAPTER 1
ESCAPE

The room is filled with smoke, and there are men drinking and gambling. The only person I recognize is my father. I am trying to escape, running from room to room, but no one is helping me. Instead, they are injecting me with needles so that I am drugged and they can take advantage of me—sexually, of course. I look to my dad for help, but he just looks at me and continues to walk around the room nonchalantly. He allows this behavior to go on because he is high as a kite off crack cocaine. The men hold me down and undress me. Kicking and screaming, I try to resist, but I am slowly becoming weak from the drugs they injected me with. The room starts to spin, and everything around me is becoming blurry, no matter how hard I try to focus. My thighs are being forcefully spread open, and I can smell booze and stale cigarettes as they begin to kiss on me and roughly slam their penises into my vagina. It is painful, for I am still a little girl. I scream, *"Get the fuck out!"* so loud I wake myself up from this horrible, repetitive nightmare that I have had since I was a child.

Sometimes, I feel the force is so strong that I feel like someone really is holding me down, and I wake up fighting myself, trying to scream as loud as I can, but the words come out in the softest whisper. I feel weak and numb, as if I really were drugged. It all feels so real, yet surreal at the same time.

Do you want to know what is crazy? Both of my sisters have similar nightmares where my father allows them to be sexually abused for drugs as well. I never knew this until recently, after I shared my secret of sexual abuse. I learned that repetitive rape dreams are connected with feeling "violated" in waking life, which I had no idea about. I honestly do not have any real memory of my father allowing things like this to happen to me, but I will say this: I was violated by a very close friend whom I considered family, and I kept this a secret for nearly thirty years. I was also the closest of my sisters with my father, who has had a very serious drug addiction from the first time I can remember. I am finally addressing these issues of depression and anxiety, rape and abandonment, and so many other life struggles, and it is beyond hard. Dealing with buried secrets and current life situations has definitely made my depression and anxiety increase. The past two years have been the worst for my depression and anxiety. I am sure my most recent relationship is what brought all of these old memories to surface. At least that is when everything started to spiral downhill quickly.

When I was in fourth grade, my family and I moved from Rochester to a town called Manchester Shortsville. It was about thirty miles southeast of Rochester, in the heart of the beautiful Finger Lakes Region, which I have grown to love and appreciate. We moved here as an attempt to "start fresh" and help my dad recover from his addiction. I remember, not long after the move, we had to attend a weekly Bible study, and I was so pissed off because we were not really the churchgoing type of family. Why do we need to read the Bible just because Dad does drugs? I mean, that is the reason we were doing a Bible study. My nana's boyfriend was trying to help my dad—not to mention he was Jewish. Nothing wrong with that, but when we did go to church, we usually went to a Christian church. Maybe it does not really matter. I am no expert on religion that is for sure. I consider myself an atheist. However, that may be due to my lack of knowledge of religion. Either way, I am thankful the sessions did not last long, but that is only because my father's recovery did not last long. Before the relapse we also had to attend Al-Anon meetings while my parents attended Narcotics Anonymous (NA) in a separate room. My parents would drop us off in some small, dusty room that smelled like coffee and cigarettes.

There was a large conference table, which was marked with carved initials and other teenage graffiti on it. There was a chalkboard on the wall, and the lights were dim. My sisters and I would be left sitting in a room with a strange woman who tried to get us to open up about dad's addiction and how it made each of us feel through these stupid games. So we were sitting there, drawing sad stick figures and writing words like *sad, angry, alone* on a piece of paper to stick in a hat so she could read our answers out loud and discuss our feelings. The first few times, we would not say a word. We would just listen as she would say things like, "It's OK to feel sad" and "None of this is your fault." The three of us hated it, and we would never discuss how we really felt once we left the room. It did not matter if we participated or not because, like everything else, this was short-lived. I was glad it was short-lived because it was so quiet and depressing every single time on the drive home. I would just sit in the back seat and gaze out the window, wondering why the entire family had to be dragged into this shit just because one person had a problem. My sisters would sit in silence, and my parents would either bicker or discuss their meeting. Either way, it was all just bullshit. We were just going to go to a meeting, and nothing would change. Dad would disappear for days at a time, and that was when Mom was fun. Everyone was in a better mood when he was not around.

Although Mom's efforts were intended to be good, my dad was still addicted to crack cocaine. It did not matter where we moved. If an addict wants a drug, he will find a way to get it, believe me. He had stayed sober for a few months, sometimes even a year at a time. However, once he was into drugs again, you could always tell because things would change. So here we were, living in this new trailer they bought, along with a new car, and months later, shit started to hit the fan. Mom and Dad were always arguing over money or him missing dinner or, in some cases, not coming home at all for days at a time. My sisters and I used to have to hide our clothes when she took us shopping. Mom would say, "Now, only show your father one outfit," when in reality, we would have two or three outfits each. As a child, I thought this was fun; my sisters and I thought it was a sneaky game. However, the older I got, the more I realized that it was actually sad. My Mom had to hide the fact that she was buying us school clothes or a toy or anything really. It is a parent's job to buy school clothes and provide for their child, so why should this be a secret? Oh, that is right, because we should not be wasting money on providing for the children when we could be drinking and smoking crack. Right, Dad?

ESCAPE

Being exposed to a drug addict and drug dealers from a very young age caused me to be a very paranoid little girl. I have had several instances where drug dealers were watching my sisters and I play, or just sitting near our home, watching the house. I remember the very first time this happened; I was about twelve years old. It was not long after our move to our new, "safe" neighborhood. We were having movie night; Mom and my sisters made popcorn and were about to watch *Friday the 13th*, which was a horror flick about a serial killer. Dad passed out on the floor with a rifle next to him. Mom made him shove it under the couch so it was not out in the open, but we all knew it was there, and just the sight of it was scary. Why did he sleep with a rifle? We lived in the country, for crying out loud. Cows and cornfields surrounded us. It was pitch black outside and even inside, because Mom was about to start our scary movie. Suddenly, there were high beams in our driveway, lighting up the whole trailer. Mom tiptoed to the window and peeked out through a tiny opening in the blinds. All she could see was a figure of a man with what appeared to be a pistol in his hand, and from the glare, she could see that it was a red sports car. She immediately started waking my dad up. I was sitting there, my heart racing so fast, afraid of what would happen next. It took Mom what seemed like an hour to wake him up because he was knocked out cold. Who wouldn't be, after being awake and partying for three days straight?

Once she finally woke him, he grabbed his rifle and runs to the door. As soon as he turned on the porch light, the car squealed out of the driveway, kicking up dust and stones. Immediately, my little sisters started crying. I just hugged them, trying to be strong for them, although my eyes were tearing up as well. I had no idea what was going to happen. This was all so scary.

Immediately Mom and Dad started arguing. We later found out that Dad owed money to the dealer, and they were coming to the house just to scare him so he would pay up, or else his family would be in jeopardy. Little did I know that this was only the beginning of learning what it was like to live with a drug addict. Honestly, I still cannot grasp the concept of why people do or say the things they do while they are on drugs. Or why they continue doing drugs when they slowly lose everything and everyone around them.

Over the years, there have been several instances when my family and I have been watched or even approached, in some cases, by the drug dealers. I began to become very paranoid and did not like being home alone at a young age, but Mom was always working to try to make ends meet since Dad was blowing his money, literally. I would call her, scared to death, begging her to come home. I would stay away from the house or have someone with me when I was there so that I was not alone. As much as I looked over my shoulder and paced around, you might have thought I was the one on drugs.

This behavior went on for several years. We lost our vehicle because it was repossessed. We had to move from the trailer because the bills were not being paid, and the drug dealers were watching our every move. We would be playing and notice random people watching us. My mom would make us come inside; then she would call my dad. She usually had to find money or borrow money so he could go pay the dealers, and then they would disappear for a while. Eventually, my mother decided she had enough of his behavior, and she no longer wanted us exposed to it, so she made him go to rehab, and the four of us moved into a house in town.

My father has been in and out of rehabs my entire life. If anything, I think these places enable the drug addicts even more. Why should you be able to go to a place, live, and eat rent free? Of course, people are kicked out of rehab if they relapse or do not follow the rules, but they are *always* allowed back. So what does that teach anyone? Maybe if he were homeless, he would get his shit together if he knew he would not always have somewhere to run to. To top it off, my dad is a veteran, so he gets monthly paychecks for having post-traumatic stress disorder (PTSD). Each month, he gets close to $3,000, and it is gone within days due to his addiction. It was not always like this. He did work when I was younger, but now he is so far gone, he does not work, and he just runs the streets, staying up for days. I always thought he would get better. I lost hope years ago. When my nana passed away, he promised he would finally get sober, but if anything, he has only gotten worse. Before her death, he would be sober for an entire year at times. He would always end up relapsing, but for the past several years, there has really been no period of sobriety. He is just gone. Just when you think he cannot get much worse, he does. The things he has done the past few years are even more horrific than the things he has done in the past, including stealing from his children. Yes, my father has stolen from all three of his children. He has stolen money, jewelry, TVs, and furniture from my sisters and me through the years. Moreover, he has never apologized. He is a coward, and he would rather disappear for months and then show up unexpectedly, acting as if nothing ever happened.

One year I took a trip to Myrtle Beach with my boyfriend Alex and my daughter, Carly. When I came home, I immediately noticed money missing from my bedroom. I had a baby bottle from my daughter's baby shower, and it was filled with change. This was hidden in my bedroom closet underneath some clothes. Therefore, someone was searching through my home while I was gone. Immediately, I felt uneasy and betrayed. I began searching around to see if anything else had been taken from my home that I may not have immediately noticed, and that is when I discovered that all of the rolled change missing from the top of the fridge. I am not positive about the amount. It may have been a hundred bucks in quarters or something around that amount. The amount is not even an important factor in this situation—not to me, anyway. What mattered was which family member was in my house stealing from me when I put my trust in them? While we were away, the only people who had access to my home were Alex's parents, his niece, and my father.

Clearly, the blame had to be placed on someone, and my father happens to be a master manipulator, something I failed to recognize over the years. I know I should have known right away it was my dad, especially since he lied about even being in the house. And because he has stolen from my sisters, why wouldn't he steal from me? The longer I was home, the more I noticed that more things were missing, such as the TV and a few of his belongings that he was storing at my house. Therefore, I confronted him, and he admitted taking those things and selling them for drugs, but he refused to admit he stole any money. He even went as far as saying he would take a lie detector test. I lied to him and told him he would have to. I was bluffing, but clearly, so was he. He knew that was impossible. The shitty thing is that since I did not want to believe my father would do this to me, I blamed Alex's niece. Alex and I would argue; of course, he would defend his niece, and I'd defend my father. Alex would say, "Kali has no reason to steal; my parents give her everything and anything she needs" (which is true; his parents raised Kali, and they spoiled her), but I'd say things like, "She is sixteen. She probably just wanted money to get drunk or something." This created a huge family blowout though. At the time, Alex was paying Kali's phone bill; they were really close, and Alex completely cut her off, took her off the phone plan, and stopped talking to her for months. He told her once she admitted taking to stealing from us, then he would add her back onto his phone plan. The confusing part was that Kali refused to take a lie detector test, unlike my father, who acted as if he had no problem taking one. Meanwhile, my dad was still coming around, acting as if nothing ever happened. It took me a long time to realize that most likely it was my dad who had stolen the money.

I mean, the day I flew home, he was at my door begging for money, and I refused to give it to him. He was high as a kite, and he was acting weird. I came home to my dog's cage full of piss and shit, when Alex's parents were caring for the dog the entire time. I remember I was scrubbing the cage, and my father was eager to help. Since when? My theory is that the dog was nervous or barking when he was in my home stealing; maybe my dad kicked the cage or something. The dog's water bowl was spilled over, and the cage was a complete mess. Why is my father trying to help clean it up and beg me for money when I just told him someone stole from me? He did not care. He wanted his next high, and that is all he cared about.

I have dealt with this behavior for nearly forty years now. Well, I am almost forty, so I have dealt with it for about thirty years. As I mentioned, there has been no time of sobriety for him. He is gone. You can see the difference physically and mentally. It is clear he has zero fucks to give. My sisters have not talked to my father in years, and I finally cut ties with him this year. This was painful for me. It is a very difficult decision to make to cut ties with your father while he is still living when so many other people would love the chance to have relationships with their fathers.

I have no idea where he is or how he is. I hear sirens; I check the news to see if he was involved. I see an accident; I pull over to see if it is his vehicle. It would not be the first time I read about him in the headlines. His name and picture were blasted all over the news when he hit a little girl crossing the road; he has totaled three cars so far. In the last car wreck, he broke several ribs, and no one even knew he was in the hospital until I called him. Of course, I went to the hospital and drove him to my mom's the day he was released. My mom and I called into work to drive over an hour to get him. He told me he fell asleep at the wheel and hit a tree. I picked up the report while the nurse was assisting him, and I began to read it. It read, "High on cocaine." So I said, "Dad you were high," and he replied, "No, sweetheart, I fell asleep at the wheel, I promise you." He kept rambling on and on, stating that he fell asleep. He said he was tired and stayed in a hotel the previous night to sleep for a few hours and then awoke after a few hours of sleeping and passed out at the wheel.

Eventually, I cut him off. I said, "Well, it says right here, you were high on cocaine." He acted surprised, and I was heated. Lies. Lies. Lies. When will they end? Not only did we run to his rescue as always, but we also supported him, took care of him, bought his cigarettes, fed him, and gave him a place to stay, and he never even acknowledged it. No thank-you, no apology, no Nothing. It becomes exhausting after a while. I was constantly making sure he was OK when the reality is that he has never made sure I was OK.

My father was also recently in the news for mugging a woman at the local library. I found out about this one before it hit the news, though, when an undercover cop showed up at my house looking for him. The cop showed up wearing a sweatshirt and khaki pants. No car was on site, and he had his lip packed with Copenhagen. He quickly flashed his badge on my front steps, and it was back in his pocket before I opened the door. I stepped out onto my porch, and he started asking questions about my dad's whereabouts and his contact information. I didn't even have my dad's phone number. I deleted it because I was sick of him selling his phone to dealers and constantly changing his number. Not to mention the dealers would have access to all of his contacts and pictures, and I decided I no longer wanted to be a part of that lifestyle. The whole night, I was sick to my stomach, wondering how he could do that to someone, but then my crazy mind started wondering, *What if that wasn't even a real cop?* He introduced himself as Officer Dan; he gave no business card or any other information, and I had given him my aunt's address because that is where I heard he was staying. Not to mention, he was texting on his phone while he was talking to me. I saw read a few of the messages that came through: "Is he there?" and "Did you check River Road?" Hours later, it dawned on me that my mom used to live on River Road. I called her immediately, nervous that it was a dealer just trying to get information to his whereabouts. I knew I was not going to sleep that night. Six long hours later, I called the local police department, asking if they knew of the situation. They confirmed that it was a real undercover cop, and they had arrested my dad. Thank God; I was so relieved.

Not only is it embarrassing to have the same last name as my father, but it also is sad to hear these stories, and I become sick to my stomach over them. I could not sleep for days when I read about the robbery. To me, that was a completely new level of addiction. This poor girl must have been scared to death; she is someone's mother, daughter, and loved one. I thought to myself, *What if this happened to my children or myself?* I had to cut ties.

CHAPTER 2

UNWANTED TOUCHES

The sexual abuse I had kept secret occurred between the ages of six and thirteen. The very first time I told anyone what had happened to me, I was thirty-seven. I kept this inside me for nearly twenty years. That is a long time to keep a secret. I hid behind a smile very well. Now, I have almost forty years of sadness, anger, and heartbreak built up in me. Some days, I feel like I want to end it all. Instead, I am trying my hardest to overcome this wide range of emotions and am learning how to deal with them.

Any sexual assault is horrible. No one deserves to be violated in this way, especially a child, and when it is someone you know, it is even harder to deal with. Yes, I knew the person. He was my age; I referred to him as my "cousin," and we spent a lot of time together. He always made it clear he was my "protector," never letting boys flirt with me or date me. It now makes sense why he acted that way. It did not make sense to me when I was an innocent little girl. I was young and naive. I thought he truly wanted what was best for me. I did not know that what he really wanted was to have me to himself. He disgusts me so much now I am not even going to give him a name, not even a fake name. He knows who he is.

When this abuse first started happening, I was only six. I would wake up to him fondling me or kissing my face and neck. But there are a few times I remember clearly as day when I was older, and I am pretty sure it is because I was going through hormonal changes; things just started to feel different.

One night, my mom and his mom were going out for the night, and I had to spend the night at his house. So it was him and I all alone in the living room, and it was dark. He was on the couch, and I was on the floor. We were watching a movie. I rolled my back to him and shut my eyes to start to rest. All of a sudden, I could hear his windbreaker pants slither onto the floor next to me, and then he spooned me. I instantly felt sick and began having flashbacks from the prior times when I was younger. I shut my eyes tighter, pretending I was passed out, hoping it would end there, and hoping this was a bad dream. My heart was racing as I kept trying to think that he would not dare do this now that we were older, right? *Wrong.* His hands wandered up my shirt, and he kept touching my breasts. I felt so dirty and gross, but I did not want to move. I had boobs now, and when he ran his fingers across my nipples, they became hard. I did not like this new feeling, and I felt like I was going to puke. I don't know why I didn't I scream, "Get the fuck out of here!" like I kept imagining. Maybe if I made a sound, he would have stopped. On the other hand, maybe if I yelled, his stepdad would have come down the stairs. I do not know. I will never know because I was silent as he put his hands down my pants and touched my vagina with his fingers. Slowly moving his fingers back and forth, he was breathing heavily as he kissed the back of my neck. It gave me the chills, but I tried not to move. When he was finished fondling my breasts and penetrating my vagina with his fingers for his own pleasure, he slowly crept back to the couch, and all I heard was a bunch of noise and then a slow moan. I later learned this was called masturbating. I was numb. I rolled over as the tears rolled down my face. I did not even move. I just lay there, letting the tears hit the pillow and dry on their own.

The next morning came, and he acted as if nothing happened, so I had to, right? I mean, whom was I going to tell? My mom refers to his mom as her sister. I call his mom my aunt, for crying out loud. I refer to him as my cousin. Is this incest? I know we are not blood related, but that is what I have always known him as since birth—yes, we have known each other for that long. So, I tried hard to act the same as I did the previous day. On the outside, everything seemed to appear fine. I still laughed and played hide-and-seek and with him and all the other neighborhood children. Inside, though, my stomach was shaking all day, and I had no appetite. I did not want anyone to know what had happened because I felt so dirty. This sickening behavior went on for several years. Some instances I remember clear as day. I can remember how I felt, which house I was in, the scent of him, and many other disturbing details. Other instances I recall waking up to him groping me, and I'd just roll over, pretending I was still asleep; he would then go away or stop for a little bit. Eventually, I did not even pretend to roll over in my sleep because all that did was prolong things. He would just move quickly, wait a few minutes, and begin to touch me again. Therefore, I learned to just lay there "asleep" and let him do his thing so he would go away. The abuse stopped when we moved from Rochester to Manchester/Shortsville, and then I no longer had to see him. Maybe that is why I thought I could just forget about him. Let me tell you, it does not work that way.

About twelve years later, my boyfriend and I were going to have a fun night out with my mom while his mom watched our daughter Carly. We planned to spend the night at her house since we were going out to a bar, and our drive was over an hour away. At the time, my mom lived in Spencerport, New York, which is in the suburbs of Rochester, and Scott and I lived with his parents in Naples, New York, which was in the Finger Lakes region. It was a long drive, but I was excited to spend time with my mom.

I remember walking into my mom's kitchen. I gave her a hug and kiss, and immediately I got the chills as I looked up to see who was sitting at her kitchen table. Yes. It was him. The boy who once abused me was sitting there as a young man, and he was beyond excited to see me. Once again, I had to act as if everything was OK As he quickly stood up and gave me a big tight hug and kiss on the cheek, while saying he missed me, I tried to smile, though I had a million thoughts running through my head. I was not even sure what I was feeling at the moment because all of these emotions came rushing back. I quickly snapped out of my thoughts, and I introduced Scott to the pervert as I pretended to be extra happy. I wanted to appear extra happy so he would know that what he did had no effect on me. Once they were introduced, the pervert started asking

Scott all sorts of questions: "What do you do for a living? How long have you been together? Are you going to marry my cousin?" He informed Scott that he was just "looking out for me like always."

The questions started to sound like background noise after a while. I started to feel sick to my stomach, and I wanted to scream, "None of your fucking business, you pervert!" Instead, I smiled and jokingly punched him in the arm, saying, "OK, enough questions, let's drink a beer." Yep. I decided I had to be wasted that night and keep my mouth *shut*. So that is exactly what I did. I drank beers and took several shots until I passed out. I kept Scott close to me all night so there was no room for an opportunity for anyone to take advantage of me. I was not letting that happen again. I am much older now, so I am not sure he would attempt it. All I know is that seeing him and hearing him act as if nothing ever happened was sickening. I felt like I was being kicked in the stomach the entire night. All these years had gone by, and I had not thought much about him and all of the unwanted touches. Seeing him brought back all the horrible flashbacks that I had blocked out for so long. I thought because I did not associate with him anymore, I could just get over it. Block it out of my head like it never happened. This happened decades ago now; shouldn't I be fine?

Clearly, even though I did not think it bothered me, it absolutely did. I even wrote about it a few times. Here is a poem called "Mommy, Please Don't Go." I often used writing as a coping mechanism when I was younger. I may have been sixteen when I wrote this, so it might not be the best poem, but it definitely describes what I was going through at the time.

Mommy, Please Don't Go

Please don't go, Mommy.
Don't leave me here to be abused. I know you do not have a clue.
Otherwise, you wouldn't leave me here, just so others can be amused.
It is getting dark, and it is late, but before the night is over,
It...will...happen.
I will sleep, and he will creep,
Down my pants and up my shirt.
He will suffocate me with his weight.
Then he will masturbate and pass out,
like...nothing...ever...happened.

This pretty much describes how it happened every single time. This poem is a cry for her not to leave me alone with him to be abused again. In reality, it did not matter because sometimes she was right there in the same room, asleep on the couch. Crazy, right? My mom was in the same room. This kid just did not give a shit. Therefore, no matter what, it was bound to happen. He would find a way to get near me no matter what.

Unfortunately, he was not the only pervert to touch me in unwanted places. There were two more boys. One was my childhood best friend's brother, which occurred during the same timeframe as the other pervert, and the other was a teenage boy at a party in Naples, who was apparently known for touching girls and having sex with them after they get wasted at parties. I did not know this because it was about a year after I moved to Naples. There was a bunch of us at a house party. I was with my boyfriend Scott, but I passed on the couch, and I woke up to a stranger touching my breasts. I felt that I was being touched all over, but I was so out of it. Everything was a blur because I was drunk. He had his hand on my breasts, I woke up, and he quickly walked away. I woke up, stumbled to find Scott, and made him come to bed with me. Of course, I did not mention anything to anyone. I did not want to cause a scene at my first party as the new girl. I figured as long as I kept Scott by my side the rest of the night, everything would be OK, and this would not happen again. I found out years later the same boy did this to my sister Cass, as well as many other girls. He even had sex with some of them because the girls were completely wasted. I would hear stories of them saying they did not remember anything, or some would say they woke up naked and noticed him leaving the room. Nothing was ever reported, though, because everyone was drunk and too scared to tell. I did not say anything to a soul for decades, and he did far worse things to other girls—one being my sister. What a sick world we live in. Children need to know this behavior is not OK and should not be tolerated or accepted. If we do not speak up, this sickening behavior continues. Do not be ashamed just because you may have been drinking illegally. This is your body. *No one* should touch it if it is unwanted. Even if you are drinking, you do not deserve to be abused in any way.

Over the years, I learned that holding these secrets only made things worse for me. All I was doing was avoiding dealing with the situation. I felt ashamed and dirty, as if it was my fault. For years, I never realized that because my breasts were always being fondled unwantedly, that once I became intimate, I absolutely hated my breasts being sucked on, kissed, or even touched. The second someone touched them, I'd quickly move their hand and tell them I don't like it, without any explanation. This was a mood killer for some. Actually, it even killed my mood sometimes. I felt so dirty when someone touched me, and I never realized the reason why until many years later, when I started to put everything together. I was associating all of the unwanted touches to my breasts with the same stimulation I felt when someone who loved me attempted to touch me. I would immediately freeze up. I was weird about my nipples being touched, to the point that I still, to this day, sleep with a bra on. I don't want my nipples touching my T-shirt or any surface that will cause them to be stimulated when I do not want them to be. It sounds absolutely crazy, I know. According to my therapist, she says it makes perfect sense, and that the way I feel is a symptom of PTSD. It has been very hard to overcome the feeling. I have slowly learned that it is OK to feel loved and allow your lover to show you how he appreciates your body. I do not need to feel dirty because I am engaging in the situation with someone I love, and it is not being forced. I had to learn not to associate every touch of intimacy with the unwanted touches of these other perverts. It was not until I was in my midthirties that I even enjoyed nipple stimulation.

Keeping my secrets and burying the emotions I was feeling was only prolonging the psychological healing process. I always thought I was protecting my mom and my family. Although we were not blood related, I still thought of him as family. We were the same age, went to the same school, and lived near one another. There was no way I could share my secret. I am positive that children in a similar situation have many of the same thoughts and feelings I have experienced or continue to experience. I want you to know that you are not alone, and you should not keep secrets like this. Tell your story so you can begin to heal, so hopefully you can prevent this from happening to others; I have always carried guilt for that as well. I know that this person has done jail time for sexually assaulting two other young girls, and I have wondered if maybe this could have been prevented, had he been confronted at a younger age. Maybe he would have gotten help or been punished for his behavior. I know that *none* of his actions are my fault. They are his fault entirely, and I will no longer blame myself, even though I feel sorry for the other victims. I have never confronted my perpetrator, and I do not plan to, but I am still able to start healing now that I am talking about my feelings and finding ways to handle my emotions. Yes, I will admit, since I started talking about the things that have happened, I have had several nightmares and flashbacks, but that is all part of the healing process. None of this has been easy, but I know I am taking a step in the right direction. Once I deal with the problem, I can put this chapter to rest for once and for all.

CHAPTER 3

ABANDONMENT

It was not long after my sixteenth birthday when my sisters and I were ripped from our home. Cass and I were shipped off to my aunt Roxanne and Tom's house, but unfortunately my middle sister, Donna, was not sent with us. Instead, she was sent off to rehab, which I learned at a later date. Once again, I was left with so many unanswered questions. Where were Mom and Dad? The real question was, where is Mom? At this point, we were used to Dad being gone for days or weeks at a time. Mom was always there for us though. She was either working or home with us, trying to make the best of everything—playing kickball with our friends, having movie nights, wrestling in the snow. All of the things most parents do with their children.

This move happened so fast, I have no recollection of how it even occurred. I do not remember packing, or the long ride to their house, or anything to deal with that day. I could not tell you how we even arrived there. I think my aunt and uncle picked us up, but it is all such a blur. I believe we were told to pack our clothes because Mom was in the hospital and we were staying with my aunt for a few days. It turned into a few years. I was told Mom had a breakdown, but I honestly do not remember witnessing any sort of breakdown. What I do remember is that she had a new boyfriend whom I *hated*, and I assumed she just chose him over us. My sisters assumed the same thing. I am pretty positive our assumptions were not far off, since we later found out Mom was a cokehead with her new cokehead boyfriend for several years.

So here sat Cass and I, sitting at a table of strangers who cooked a full-course meal nightly. What was all this food, and why were we eating together at the table? Why were there seven Maltese dogs barking at our feet? Why were there cats, and why did it smell like bacon in there all the time? Family dinners did not happen in my home, and when they did, it was as lax as can be. Eating in the living room while watching TV or shoving food down our throats quickly so we could run in the streets with our friends. Eating ramen noodles or whatever we could cook for ourselves while Mom was working and Dad was out smoking crack. We did not sit and have conversations about how our day was or what we did. Was this a game of twenty questions? Were they just trying to get to know us? Turns out it was not a game of twenty questions. These people were genuine, loving people, and that is how it was for many years. And the bacon smell—that was just the wood stove.

Another shock that came along with this move was…rules! We now had rules. What the fuck? I was sixteen. Why I have a bedtime now, homework time, and a curfew? What was a curfew? This was all too much to handle. When you go from being able to do what you want and roam the streets with your friends and stay out when you want to, even if it is a school night, and, all of a sudden, there is structure, it makes you want to lash out and become angry. I mean I was already angry that my parents did not want my siblings and me, and I was even angrier that we were separated. I was staying with the people I saw at family picnics once a year. Who were these people anyway? All I knew was that Roxanne was Dad's sister, and Tom was her boyfriend who was old enough to be her father, literally. The man was my nana's age.

It was not long after this move that I was put on Zoloft, which is a depression medication. I did not feel depressed. I felt angry and sad. What do I truly know about what I felt or what I needed at that point? I was only sixteen years old. So, of course, I thought I handled everything fine. I struggled with the thought of being on depression medication for years, and then I would just randomly stop taking the pills the second I felt less emotional or that I no longer needed a "happy pill," as I referred to it. Let me tell you, it is not a good idea to start and stop any prescribed medication without the consent of your physician, unless you want to be on even more of an emotional roller coaster. At sixteen, all I knew, or thought I knew, is that I did not need a prescription just because I had fucked-up parents. I also thought I had to be strong and set an example for my little sister. Therefore, if it meant acting like everything was OK when it really was not, then that is what I did. I was always the protector. I needed to make sure she had everything she needed, and I needed to make her laugh so she was not sad. I needed to comfort her.

It was during this time in my life that I started to feel many emotions such as pain, anger, and embarrassment. In the beginning, my anger was mainly at times when rules were trying to be enforced or when I did not get my way. After a while, I was angry for being abandoned by my parents, separated from my sisters, and much more. At my old home, I had no curfew. My mom worked sixty hours a week, and my dad was almost never around—which meant I could have parties and drink and stay out late. Jesus, Cass was six years younger than I was, and she was roaming the streets at 11:00 p.m. with the other neighborhood kids. It is no wonder Donna ended up in rehab. She was tripping on acid, walking all over town with her friends at the young age of fourteen. I remember one time, the cops were called because she was missing, and this is when kids did not have cell phones or anything, so there was never a way to get ahold of us. Anyway, the cops found her at the local playground with a group of kids who were all tripping. When the police officer was talking to her, she asked him why his face was dripping on the floor. Clearly, his face was not melting on the floor. Apparently, acid makes you do and see some fucked-up shit that is not really happening. She was hallucinating. I am not exactly sure what happens to you because I have never done acid; all I knew was that she was acting crazy and talking crazy. I have never done acid.

I did try hallucinogenic mushrooms, also called "'shrooms," my senior year, so I guess that would almost be the same experience. I am pretty sure I tried them on the day I was supposed to graduate. Yes, I did graduate high school. I just did not walk across the stage with my fellow classmates. Why? Because no one was around to come watch me graduate. I was the first one in the family to receive my diploma, and *no one* could come to my graduation. So I decided that I was not going to humiliate myself and walk across the stage alone while everyone else had family supporting them on their big day taking photos of this ceremony that is supposed to be a huge milestone in your life. This was the day your life changes; it is time to grow up and become an adult pursue your dreams and become more responsible. Maybe this is exactly why I wanted to get so wasted. It seems to be a pattern of mine, which I am recently realizing. Whenever I am feeling betrayed or abandoned or hurt in any sort of way, I immediately want to numb myself. Nevertheless, graduation day was the *first* and *last* time I ever tried hallucinogenic mushrooms. My experience was not fun at all. Well, let's be honest. It was, and it was not. It was fun because I felt great, and it increased my tolerance for drinking beer, and we all know I love beer. So I did a shit ton of keg stands at a graduation party I attended. It was after the keg stands when I started to feel the side effects from the mushrooms. We ended up going to a party with about four hundred people, and I felt great on the ride there. I believe the ride to the party was when I started to hallucinate. I felt like I was floating through the air, and I was in the back seat of the Jeep with the windows down, wind blowing through my hair, and the lights from the radio were all coming in my direction like a disco ball. I felt untouchable. I wanted to jump out of the car; I thought I could fly. Thankfully, my boyfriend Scott would not let me open the doors and attempt to fly. When we arrived at the party, my friends kept me locked in the Jeep because, all of a sudden, I could not be around this many people while I was tripping my face off. I remember petting a friend's hair, telling her it felt like cornhusks. When we stepped out of the Jeep, everything looked as if it was spinning. I had all of these people talking in my face, and it was as if I was looking into a fun house mirror. My friends put me back in the Jeep because I was freaking out with all of these people around. The crowd was overwhelming for me, but I did not want to be forced to stay in the Jeep while all of my friends were at this party. I tried kicking my way out of the Jeep.

ABANDONMENT

After many unsuccessful attempts to escape, my friends thought it would be best to get me home, which I am thankful for, since I was still in rough shape for the next several hours. I remember watching *Sabrina the Teenage Witch*, which totally freaked me out because there was a cat on the show that talked to humans. The cat freaked me out for sure.

The next morning, I saw my muddy footprints all over the inside rooftop of the Jeep. I thought to myself, "What the fuck happened?" Therefore, I have never tried shrooms again, and I never will.

I guess you could say I started drinking around the age of fourteen. Once I was separated from my family, I began to drink every weekend. Maybe this is the normal teenage thing to do, but I didn't just drink. I drank to the point where I blacked out. I don't mean a blackout once in a while; I had them often. One night, shortly after moving in with Roxanne and Tom, I ended up with alcohol poisoning, and I was still trying to drink after violently puking for several hours. It was so bad, my friends had to call my aunt and uncle, and they had to come pick me up from Manchester (my old hometown) at three thirty in the morning. They weren't too pleased. I ended up being grounded for the first time ever. This was another struggle. I had never really been disciplined my entire life, and now I was grounded. This made me so angry. I felt like my aunt hated us. Uncle Tom was pretty chill; he was always laid-back. Roxanne was strict, though, and I felt like we were in the military at times. I didn't even have a graduation party because I ended up being grounded for coming home past curfew. Who does that? Jesus, I was the first one to graduate in this family. I didn't even bother going to my graduation ceremony. The school mailed me my cap and gown and my diploma. What was the point of going? No one was coming to watch me walk across the stage anyway. I still went to other graduation parties and partied.

Obviously, Roxanne cared for us; it just took a while adjusting to this new way of living. It was an adjustment for all of us. Roxanne and Tom had always wanted children of their own, but she couldn't get pregnant. They spent thousands of dollars trying to have a baby together. Then one day, they take two young girls into their home. They didn't know the first thing about parenting or how to handle us, and we didn't know how to handle either of them or their rules.

I was always being grounded, whether it was for sneaking my sister snacks because she wouldn't eat her dinner, or coming home past curfew, or partying with my little sister, or driving her to school. Yes, driving her to school. I wasn't allowed to drive my sister to school, and if I did, Roxanne and Tom would find out right away; Uncle Tom was a school bus driver, so our bus driver would tell Tom if Cass was on the bus or not. I thought it was the dumbest rule ever, so of course I drove my little sister to school at times. Who wants to take a bus at any age, let alone take a bus when you are the new kid in town?

Over the years, Roxanne and I grew to be very close. I realized she was the one who was always there for me and that she really did care. The older I got, the more I could see how much she did for us and how she truly did care. I mean, it wasn't her responsibility to care for us. I started to love the family feeling: going to picnics, interacting with cousins and other aunts and uncles, having a normal routine in my life. It was nice to come home and know that both Roxanne and Tom would be there and that we would be having dinner together nightly. It was nice having them ask about our day and genuinely care what we did. The routine that I hated in the beginning became something that I ended up enjoying. It was nice to have stability for once in my life. The shitty part is that eventually I was abandoned by Roxanne as well.

Roxanne and Tom split about three years after Cass and I moved in with them. I believe it wasn't too long after their split that Cass ended up moving to Rochester with my mom. I am not sure how this happened or why it happened, or if it was even an option for me to go, but I am pretty sure it wasn't. I had already graduated high school by this point. I had my own job and my own car and was attending the local community college, so I stayed put. Besides, I had hardly talked to my mom all these years I had been away, so why would I go back now that I was nineteen? I was old enough to be on my own. I did stay in touch with my father, though, because Roxanne was his sister, so I saw him often either at family picnics, or he would come visit.

I guess you could say I slowly started to see another side of Roxanne once she split from Tom. However, we still remained very close for at least a decade. Apparently Roxanne had been cheating on Tom. I remember the summer before she split from Tom, she said we were going on a trip to the Thousand Islands. My Papa lived in the thousand islands, so I assumed we were going to visit. I thought it was just going to be Roxanne, myself, and my boyfriend Scott, but she pulled over a few miles after we left home to "pick up a friend" (Ron). This friend was my age. This made me slightly uncomfortable. I was living with Uncle Tom and Roxanne, and now we were heading to the Thousand Islands as "couples," but Tom was not included. It just felt wrong—not to mention the age difference. She went from dating someone twenty years older than her to someone who is twenty years younger than her. I am not sure what she was dealing with that made her act this way all of a sudden. Maybe Tom wasn't giving her the attention she needed. Which, in my opinion is not a valid reason to cheat. Either way, this new guy was a scumbag. I remember talking shit to him at a bonfire one night, and he gave me a black eye. I said something sarcastic to him, and he was offended, so he hauled off and punched me right in the eye. That must have made him feel manly, to hit a young girl with a closed fist and give her a black eye in front of several people at a party.

The shitty part is that everyone was so afraid of Ron that no one even hit him back. They just picked me up from the ground and made sure we were separated the rest of the night. Roxanne and Ron dated for a very brief time. Ron apparently had a girlfriend, and when she found out about Roxanne, she showed up at our apartment and kicked her ass. That was actually embarrassing. I went to school with his girlfriend, and one night she showed up at my aunt's apartment (because it was after she moved out from Tom's), and the two of them fought in the gravel driveway while a handful of other young teens watched. Who was this lady turning into? How embarrassing to have a bunch of teenagers in your driveway while your aunt fights one of them. They both fought like girls, slapping and pulling hair. It was dumb, and everyone was cheering them on. I refused to step out on the balcony and watch.

Not long after her fling with Ron, she started dating another man, whom I later found out was Ron's stepdad. Was this turning into a soap opera or what? Roxanne dated Joe for several years though—at least ten years. I am not positive. I actually liked Joe. He was a good guy. He had a terrible temper at times but overall was a good guy. Eventually, they had two boys of their own. She had her firstborn just three weeks after I had my first daughter. She had complications with both and had them both prematurely, but they are strong and healthy now. Being pregnant at the same time brought us even closer. We spent a lot of time together. Roxanne was like a mother to me for a solid ten-plus years. We had family dinners together a few times a week. I was at her house daily; we went on vacations together. Our children were really close for the first five years, and then we slowly drifted apart. This was tough on me in the beginning, I felt like I was losing another parent.

Roxanne hurt her back at work after having her firstborn and has been on disability ever since. She became addicted to pain pills, and now she drinks and takes pills all the time. At first, we didn't realize it was a problem; I thought she needed them for her back, and I am sure she did, but once she became addicted, she was not the same person anymore. We couldn't carry a conversation; she would just doze off midsentence, and she was doing this in front of the children. She began lying, stealing, and cheating. I no longer trusted her to watch my daughter. I did not want to know about her affairs or hear of her lies. It was best to stay distant, even though at times it was hard because I cared for her. I wanted her to do well, and I wanted her to be the person she used to be, the one I used to love and respect.

What really disgusted me and made me lose respect for her is the fact that she got into a car accident and lied to the family about it. She claimed that the other driver ran a stop sign and hit her car. She even lied about what town it was in. What was odd is that she didn't notify the family to even tell us about the accident or that her youngest was hospitalized and had a broken leg because of the accident. The only reason we found out is because my best friend, Hannah, was in the hospital and happened to see my aunt. So Roxanne told Hannah about the accident, and Hannah notified me. I thought it seemed suspicious, though, so Hannah and I did our own investigating, and I found the police article. The accident wasn't in the town she claimed it was in. Roxanne was high on pills, and the accident was her fault.

Over the years, she has been caught in several lies, she has been caught stealing from family; she has cheated on her fiancé. She is not the same person I knew who raised me. She slowly became another stranger in my life.

Roxanne was one of the most stable people in my life for several years; to watch her go downhill so quickly was devastating. To this day, we hardly speak. I see her maybe two times a year, and the only reason I even bother going to see her is so that I can see my cousins. Otherwise, I wouldn't even bother. I am pretty sure I have a family full of strangers. I can trust no one.

CHAPTER 4

CHEATERS

Each relationship is an experience, right? I believe each relationship teaches you something. From your first love, to your happily ever after, and everything in between. You learn how to love, how to communicate, how to trust, and so much more. Of course, not everything you learn is always a positive experience, but that is what helps you grow stronger as a person from the pain you endure. A good friend once told me, "People come into your life for a reason, a season, or for life." Therefore, I try to keep that in mind, especially when people are leaving my life for one reason or another. It took me until now to realize the effect each of my relationships have had on me. My very first boyfriend: Zane, cheated on me. At the time, of course, I was devastated because he was my first true love. My first kiss, the one I lost my virginity to. We dated for three and a half years. We were going to get married. (Not really.) I was only fifteen when we started dating. We were inseparable until we were permanently separated from each other when he moved out of state with his family. One day before the move, I heard a rumor that he had cheated on me at a bonfire that I was not at one night, and I did not believe the rumor. Why are girls so naive? Is it just because I loved him and trusted him? Or was he a good liar? Or maybe I didn't want to believe it. I was a teenager, so I am not sure why I would not want to believe what the entire school was talking about. Maybe it was because this was embarrassing. I had so many questions and thoughts racing through my head once again. Why would he cheat? Was I not good enough? We had sex. I did whatever he wanted. I gave up my virginity for him. Why did he go somewhere else at such a young age? Are all men just pigs? I wanted answers, and of course, I was not getting any. I was just getting promises from him over and over that these rumors were a lie: "People are jealous." He would never risk losing me to "Sarah the skank." He said, "She just wants me." These are things he said and what I believed. I thought maybe she did want him; she flirted with everyone. After all, she was the school slut.

Girls, please do not be as naive as I was. He said all these things to keep me, and it worked—for a little while anyway.

Over the years, I have learned that I give everyone the benefit of the doubt because I would like to see the good in people. I believe true love does exist, even after all of my heartbreak. I have only had four serious relationships, and not one of them was perfect—that is for sure. In fact, they were the complete opposite of perfect. All of them were long term though. After my first love, Zane, there was Scott, whom I dated on and off for about seven years. Scott and I had my first daughter, Carly, together. After Scott was Alex, whom I dated for seven and a half years; we had my second daughter, Alexa. And my last relationship was someone whom I considered my soul mate, yet it was the shortest, most toxic relationship I had ever been in. I dated very few people in between these relationships. Three people, if I am being honest. Clearly, they were either rebounds, or one of us was not interested in a relationship at the time.

I will tell my story about each relationship, but I just want to point out the fact that how you are treated in a relationship does shape you and has a huge impact on you, whether you realize it or not, especially when you continuously experience infidelity. Being cheated on repeatedly over time affects your self-esteem and self-perception. I never realized that I was settling for less than I deserved or putting up with more than I should. You need to know that it is *not* OK for your partner to be unfaithful. In my opinion—true love or not—kick his ass to the curb, and find someone who will appreciate you and give you the love and respect you deserve. After all, if you do not respect yourself, who will? I want people who experience this to know they need value themselves, or no one else will. It may sound cliché, but it is 100 percent true. If someone does not give you their all, then do not settle for less.

All of my relationships have been long-term, yet toxic in one way or another. I started dating Scott not to long after I was swept from my home to live with my unknown relatives. I had recently ended my relationship with Zane due to his repetitive cheating and lies, besides we were also living states apart at this point. I met a girl named Danica when I first moved to Naples. She was one of my first friends. She introduced me to Scott and Noah, and the four of us spend the entire summer together hiking and partying. Eventually Danica disappeared, and it was the three of us partying and doing teenage shit together: going mudding through the woods in Noah's Jeep, getting high, and drinking beers. Eventually Noah moved to North Carolina to be with some chick who was at least ten years older than he was, but we stayed in touch over the years. Scott and I still dated; I was three years older than he was, so I graduated before him, and I was off to the local community college while he was still in high school. I ended up moving in with Scott and his parents before high school was over for me because my aunt was so strict and always trying to give me a curfew. I worked my ass off my senior year. I hardly participated in any senior milestone events, such as the senior ball or senior prom or even the senior trip. I could not even tell you where the trip was. I was that uninvolved with school activities. I only cared about working and partying.

When I was twenty-three, I ended up pregnant with Carly, and Scott was only twenty. He broke up with me. Yes, while I was pregnant. He ignored me for a while. I had to call his job to get in touch with him for doctors' appointments. I moved out of his parents' house immediately and into my mom's, with whom I'd hardly had a relationship the past ten years. I had nowhere to go. I worked as a server, and eventually Scott came around to visit a few times while I was pregnant. Once I had the baby, we tried to make our relationship work so I moved back in with him and his parents. However, it did not last long. I heard that Scott was with my best friend while I was pregnant but, of course, I did not believe it. Why would I? I was young. I was trying to be a mom and have a family, so maybe I just did not want to believe it for that reason alone. I felt like I needed to make it work. I had a little girl. I knew what it was like to have a part-time father, and I did not want that for my child. I wanted my girl to have both parents, something neither Scott nor I had growing up, so you would think he would have wanted the same thing. The last thing I wanted in the world was to be a single mother, but eventually, hanging onto something that is not there becomes exhausting. I had decided it was best to go. I had put up with more than enough, and it was time for me to escape. I was sick of the lies, sick of trying to create something that did not exist. I was tired of competing with all of these other girls. My focus now was this precious little girl. I did not have time to worry about with whom her dad was cheating on me while I was home cooking and cleaning, trying to make ends meet.

I think in each of my relationships, I went through a few boiling points before I finally exploded and decided it was time to go for good. I think these toxic relationships are equivalent to a volcano. You know how the lava is flowing, yet it is extremely hot and dangerous, and occasionally it erupts. When a volcano erupts, the molten rock rises to the surface and explodes, destroying everything around it. Yep. That sums it up. I would go through these phases, and I would try so hard to create a perfect little family and be happy. Then I would be cheated on, or left home alone on an anniversary. Or out doing fun things with my girls while their dad was out partying.

I reached my boiling point with Scott soon after Carly was born. He wanted to go out one night, and we could not both go out because one of us had to stay with the baby. So I stayed, and he never came home. I only know he lied because I busted him. I had a feeling he was with Danica, so I loaded the baby in the car and drove past Danica's house while I was on the phone with him. I asked him where he was, and he said, "I'm at Johnny's." So I said, "Where's your car?" and he said, "It's here; I just didn't want to drive." As soon as I said, "Then why is your car in Danica's driveway?" he called me crazy. It was a big argument. He was flipping everything around on me, just as he always has. That is what cheaters do. They make you feel crazy, or they try to blame you for their behavior. Bottom line is, he was busted, and once again, I moved out. My heart was racing as I sped past her house. I called my mom crying my eyes out with Carly in the back seat. I drove to my mom's to vent and try to calm down. At this point, there did not need to be a discussion with Scott; I was pretty much slapped in the face once again. I was up all night with a newborn while he was five minutes away parting and fucking some whore whom I called a good friend until that night.

Over the next few days, I searched for an apartment in the *Penny Saver* and thankfully found one quickly. And just like that, I packed my bags and left his parents' house. It was just Carly and me in my very first apartment right in Naples, New York.

It was a little shit apartment, but the rent was cheap, and that was a good thing, since I had to furnish everything all on my own. I needed everything and had nothing and no one to help. I busted my ass to purchase big items like a bed, a couch, and all of the little things that add up, such as dishes, towels, groceries—the list seemed never ending. It was just a one-bedroom apartment, which was all I needed for my baby girl and myself at the time. She slept in my bed anyway, even when I finally moved into a two bedroom. Her bedroom was just a place for her to play, and she used her bed to line up all of her stuffed animals. We stayed in Naples until she was in second grade, and that is when I moved to Canandaigua, New York.

Of course, I was dumb enough to take Scott back one more time after I had moved out. It was over for good when Carly was about four years old. All I remember is that, of course, he cheated on me, and this time there was more involved. He was dealing drugs, and I found them in my daughter's diaper bag. If someone hurts me, I can handle that, but if someone puts the welfare of my daughter at risk, that will not be tolerated. He was dealing drugs with my daughter in the car. I lost my shit. I freaked out. I broke dishes, I punched walls, I hit him, I cried, I hugged him. I cried some more, and then I kicked him out. That is right; he lived with me. Get. The. Fuck. Out. This still wasn't our final goodbye, believe it or not. We had one more "hookup." We did not date; we just hooked up. This happened years after our final breakup, and it was just a one-time thing. He, of course, had a girlfriend he lived with, but I was convinced he would never change and had not changed, and I wanted to prove a point. I know that it may have been wrong, but, listen, I had my reasons. Number one, I wanted to get laid, and I wasn't the type to sleep around, so I figured if I had sex with an *ex*, then, hey, no harm done. Number two, I was so sick of his girlfriend bragging that he cheated on me with her and constantly trash-talking me. So, yes, I texted him and put the offer out there, and of course, he could not resist. So I got all dolled up, threw on some jeans and some high heels, and drove to his work, which was an hour away. We fucked in the back of his truck, and it sucked; I didn't even orgasm. I think it was the closure I needed.

For some reason, I needed to know that he had not changed and that I wasn't the reason he cheated. So many girls blame themselves; this was proof that he would cheat on anyone. I also wanted to know that if I wanted him, I could have him. I think this is a natural feeling. I think all of the emotions I went through are normal, but no one really talks about them. At the time, I just felt confused, but I have really learned so much. The fact that he cheated on me and I stayed has to do with wanting attention, feeling loved instead of betrayed. I wanted him to love me and tell me how sorry he was. The thing is, those moments I longed for were short-lived, and his behavior was repetitive. I am not going to lie; I kind of felt sorry for this current girlfriend afterward, although part of me wanted to tell her and to rub it in her face like she had mine, but I figured it wasn't worth it. At this point, I think they deserved each other. Since that day, I have never been intimate with him, and he may have asked for a hookup a time or two. (And by "may," I mean he did ask but was denied). Not going to lie—him asking to hook up was a great feeling. I think it was the simple fact that I had the power. He could not have me or hurt me anymore, and he never will have that power again.

Months after my last hookup with Scott, I hung out with Alex. He was a customer of the bank I had worked at. He was someone I had gone to school with but never really associated with. To be honest, after the first night, I am not sure why there was even another night. I remember showing up at the local pub, where we had decided to meet up at and have a drink. Of course, I was a little nervous. I had not dated anyone in so long. So I got to the pub and ordered a drink. I spotted Alex playing darts with what appeared to be his parents and a few buddies. So now I was really nervous; he had an entire posse with him, and I was all by myself. He did not even come over to say hi right away. So I was stuck sitting at the bar while the bartender hit on me the entire time. I thought, *Fuck it*; this was uncomfortable, so I did a few shots to loosen up. I often find myself looking back, wondering why I have allowed such negative behaviors in my life. I should have known that if he did not have the balls to come meet me alone or to come say hi right away, that I should have gotten up and left. I have no idea why I stayed, but I did, and eventually we started dating.

After we dated for seven months, I finally introduced him to Carly. This was the first person I had introduced her to, and she was five. I am very protective of my girls. I do not like to introduce them to anyone unless I see that the relationship will be long term. Alex and I moved to Canandaigua, and three years later, we bought a house together. As I look back, I overlooked several red flags from the start of our relationship.

From the very beginning, Alex was protective. I was not allowed to hang out with any of my guy friends. He was always jealous of everything. Why didn't I leave sooner than I did? These were clearly signs I had witnessed in my previous relationship. One morning, Alex hacked my Facebook while he was traveling. Well, he tried anyway. He was in Georgia. I was home in New York, and I received a text message reading, "Someone in Elbert, Georgia, tried to log in to your Facebook Was this you?" I messaged Alex and asked him what town he was in, and he said he was in Elbert County, Georgia, so then I asked him if he tried to log in to my Facebook. I already knew it was him; I had the proof. I just wanted to see if he would tell me the truth. Of course, he swore up and down that it was not him and he had "no reason to do that"—that is, until I sent him the screenshot stating that it was someone in Georgia, the *exact* location he was in. Come on! What are the chances it was someone else when Alex was in that county and state at the very moment this happened? I was so angry that he would lie about something so stupid. That was just one of many lies from Alex, and this was before I bought a house and stayed with him for another four years.

Sometimes I think I stayed because I was hanging onto that "family" that I wanted so badly. I loved taking family vacations, making crafts, and creating memories. These were things I did not do as a child with my family, and I wanted to give my daughter so much more than I had. Of course, at the time, that is not what I realized at all. I justified every single action, saying things like "It was just a text message" or "I shouldn't be hanging with other guys." Nevertheless, really, what was the harm? I was so faithful, and these guy friends were from high school. Most of them even had girlfriends, and we used to all hang out. I could no longer go to happy hour with coworkers if guys were going to be there. Alex was invited; what was the problem, and why did I tolerate this behavior? Ladies, if your man is insecure and questioning you, then *he* is most likely the one who is up to no good. Alex was acting this way toward me because he knew what he was doing was wrong. I have learned that cheaters tend to rationalize their behavior in their own mind so they create these hostile environments with their partner as a way to blame them for their own behavior. Deep down, I knew all of this was wrong. I would always set these milestone dates in my head. I would tell myself, "I will break up with him after our trip to Disney," or "I will break up with him after the holidays." The only person who knew I would set these dates was my best friend, Hannah. She knew I was not truly happy and that I was just comfortable. Why didn't I see it until years later?

In the last few years of our relationship, there were several instances when I would come across Alex being unfaithful. I always felt that since Alex was nice and we built this so-called family lifestyle I didn't want to just leave because of my own insecurities (or so I thought). Any one reason is reason enough to leave, which I realize now. For instance, one night Alex passed out drunk, and his phone lit up at 4:00 a.m. I rolled over, and the message just read, "Hey." The name was listed as Marty. Now, I was not the type to look through anyone's phones, especially someone I am in a relationship with. I have always thought that girls who do that shit are crazy. I feel you should trust your partner, and your partner should trust you. Otherwise, what is the point of the relationship, right? So I rolled back over and lay there. However, something in my gut thought it was odd that Marty was saying "hey" at 4:00 a.m. So I rolled back over and tried to wake Alex up so I could tell him to respond. He would not move, though. So, for the first time ever, I picked up his phone, and I wrote down Marty's number. I called Marty privately, and it turns out Marty is actually Mary. Always trust your gut. If you are feeling something is not right, most likely, you are correct. I dialed the number and heard a girl's voice: "Hey, you've reached Mary. I can't take your call right now. Please leave your name and number, and I'll call you back." Mary, who the fuck are you, and why are you texting my man at four in the morning? I lay there all night in silence, heart racing, and feeling like I was kicked in the stomach once again.

The next morning, as soon as Alex woke, I questioned him over and over again, and he swore it was Marty and that he worked with the kid. He even tried to show me a Marty whom he was friends with on Facebook, claiming it was him. Then he did the unthinkable and swore on his grandmother's grave that it was Marty. This intensified my anger quickly. Lying right to my face and swearing on your dead grandmother's grave? I threw the phone at him and shoved him so hard he fell against the washing machine. I screamed at him and told him, "I called her already. You met her in Syracuse at a bar." Of course, this is when he started stuttering and saying that his boss gave her his number and blah, blah, blah. Call me stupid, but this still was not when I left.

He convinced me that nothing happened. So I convinced myself that I had no solid proof that they were intimate. Did I really just not want to know the truth? Because I know that whether they hooked up or not, it is still considered cheating. The intent was certainly there, and he already sworn on his grandmother's grave, so clearly there was something to hide.

After Mary's text, I was not the same. I knew the relationship was shit, and it only took a few more weeks to finally be done with all of the bullshit. Just weeks later, a group of us went out to a local pub to celebrate a promotion I received at work. We were doing shots and having a good time. I am sitting at the bar talking with Alex's old roommate Mac, and I saw he was getting messages from Alex. Wasn't that odd? We were all sitting at the bar. I knew something was up. Mac could tell I was not myself either. Alex and I hardly spoke to one another when we were out. We checked in and gave a random, meaningless kiss to one another every so often. When we got home, I could see Alex's phone lighting up on the nightstand, and it was Mac. I found out Alex was texting Mac all night long begging for a former girlfriend's phone number, who happened to be at the bar that same night. I was hysterical. I didn't even wake Alex up to confront him. I think I was in shock; I was numb. I was over this behavior. I knew I deserved better. Instead, I went downstairs and talked to his friend Nate, who had spent the night at our house that night. Nate felt awful. He told me stories of how devastated he was when his ex-cheated on him because he wanted to marry her. So I could see the guilt in Nate's eyes. He felt sorry for me. If his own friends were feeling sorry for me, it must be time to go. Both of Alex's friends were sympathetic towards me that night. Nate and I shared stories of betrayal and what it does to someone. I was also impressed that Mac had refused to give Alex this girl's phone number. Alex was saying things like "She looks so hot" and "Jen and I do not even have sex anymore," and Mac's responses were "You are drunk, Alex" and "You have a good girl at home." I was honestly shocked that Mac responded the way he did. In my eyes, Alex and his friends were all male whores. The number of women they all slept with disgusted me. I could never sleep with so many partners in my life. However, I did have a new respect for Mac. He was very apologetic for Alex's behavior, and I think he knew I was finally done—emotionally checked out, anyway.

I did confront Alex, and I immediately started looking for apartments so I could move out as soon as possible. I was OK with finally leaving. I did not tell anyone though. The plan was not to tell my family or friends—with the exception of Hannah, of course—until I signed a lease and it was real. But that day didn't come as soon as I hoped for.

CHAPTER 5
TRAPPED

I was four days late on my period, and I was freaking out, but no one knew. I needed to get out of the house and clear my head. I told Alex I was going tanning when really I went to the local grocery store to purchase pregnancy tests. I may have been in denial, though, because before going to the grocery store, I did actually go to the parking lot of the local tanning place, but I could not actually force myself to go in. I knew that I was most likely pregnant because my period was *never* late. So I sat there in silence, staring through the windows as I thought to myself, *I can't go tan if I'm pregnant.* Arguing with myself in my own head, I'd think, *you're not pregnant; you're stressed.* Then I'd think, *Yes, you are pregnant, dumbass.* I just sat there debating on whether I should just go tan and calm down or whether I shouldn't tan because if I was pregnant, it could harm the baby. Eventually, I slowly backed out of the parking lot; as the tears dripped down my face, I went to purchase a pregnancy test.

I went home and took the test, and one second later, there was a pink plus sign. First reaction: Fuck my life! Why did there have to be a pink positive sign immediately? What happened to the four minutes it was supposed to take? I came out of the bathroom and told Alex and Carly, and they were both so happy. He immediately called his parents. I did not. I made an appointment with my ob-gyn, and then I called my mom and told her once it was confirmed, days later. I was in no hurry to announce this news. My dream to move out was just shattered. Everyone was so fucking happy, but no one knew what I was going through emotionally. I was not happy at all. I felt trapped. I didn't want another baby. I wanted to leave this place I used to call home and start over fresh. Just Carly and me. I wanted to be done with Alex for good and not have any ties to him. Being pregnant meant I had to stay, right? I could not have two baby daddies and be a single mom. I thought, *What a scumbag I am; I cannot take another child from her father.* So I didn't. I stayed for two more years. Two very long, very hard years. I was in robot mode. I tried hard to make it work the entire nine months of my pregnancy, and I tried even harder once my sweet baby girl was born. Do you know how hard it is to go on family vacations and host family picnics and holidays when you cannot even stand your partner? We were hosting these events and smiling and interacting with everyone, and we couldn't stand each other. We smiled with everyone else and scowled at each other. We became pretty good actors, always pretending everything was great.

He made me feel so unwanted for so many years, so why was he happy about the pregnancy? I'll tell you why. I believe it's because he thought this would save us. Well, he was partially right. The pregnancy gave us three more years together. Yet, we acted more like roommate's than lovers.

In the end, there was no intimacy; I couldn't even fake that anymore. Do you know what it feels like to have sex and feel nothing? Most of the time, I'd just say to him, "Just do it from behind." This was for two reasons: number one, I didn't have to look at him, and number two, I knew he would have an orgasm faster. Sometimes, I'd lie there and think about random things; one day, I even counted how many pumps it took him before he came (ninety-nine). No matter what, there was no emotional connection. I did not love him. I hardly liked him. Everything he did annoyed the fuck out of me. I couldn't even stand to hear him breathe.

He never gave me the time of day. We never spent quality time together. We hardly spoke. We both worked. I cooked, I cleaned, I did all of my motherly duties, and then we climbed into bed at the end of a long day and sat as far apart from each other as we could. We'd stare at our phones until the lights went out, hardly give one another a kiss goodnight, and then do the same thing over and over. Day after day. Year after year. It became exhausting, and I was emotionless.

I always felt I tried so hard, when Alex never took the time to really know much about me or participate in anything I did like to do. Alex knew that my absolute favorite thing to do was hike, and he never hiked once with me in seven and a half years. Well, we had gone to Watkins Glen State park located in New York, with me a few times as a family outing. I guess you can count that as a hike; it has several gorges, and you walk up hundreds of stairs to view several waterfalls. Nineteen to be exact. It really is pretty. The point is he knew hiking was my favorite thing to do, and he never wanted to hike with me. He knew I was into crafts, he hated crafts as well. Never made any attempt to craft with the girls and I. Meanwhile, I was doing all of his favorite things, whether I wanted to or not. I did them to try and make it work. Realizing all of this was heartbreaking. Realizing he probably couldn't tell you what my favorite meal or ice cream flavor was when I could tell you everything about him was a slap in the face. I cried myself to sleep for over a year straight before deciding that I could no longer function like a robot. Life is too short to be living some fake happy family bullshit life. I wanted to feel alive again. I wanted to be with someone who actually knew me and appreciated me for who I was.

When I told Alex I was leaving, and he cried and begged for me to stay. He swore he would change, and I almost believe he might have been for real now, but it was too late. He asked me to give him six weeks to prove that things will get better. The New Year had just passed. I told him I'd give him time to prove himself. In reality, I was already checked out. I began continuing my search for my own place. Six days later, I told him I was moving out. He was angry because I didn't give him time to prove himself. But you know what? He had seven and a half years of my life to prove himself, and the only thing he proved was what a selfish prick he is. So, it didn't matter if he was serious about changing. I am sure he did realize what a mistake he made. He even wanted to try therapy, *all the therapy in the world wouldn't help at this point.* He shouldn't have took me for granted all those years. There was no way I could stay another six months

I was in my own place with my girls less than one month later, and it was tough, but I was happier. I was beginning to feel more alive. I was doing things I had always loved but no longer did anymore, such as hike. Hiking and being in nature was my therapy; it *is* my therapy. I just love nature and to be in the woods listening to the sound of waterfalls or a creek bed, the crunching sound the leaves make as I was down the paths. The birds chirping and the chipmunks playing on the fallen trees. It is all natural beauty. Not to mention I absolutely love photography, so I am always taking tons of pictures of the beauty I am surrounded by that most people overlook, such as one lonely leaf floating down the creek, a chipmunk eating an acorn, or an up-close picture of a snail on a leaf. You can see their eyes when you zoom in. It is creepy but cool at the same time. Doing all of these things made me feel less stressed and more at peace with everything.

Even though I was happier for the most part, the decision to leave was still very hard on me. I did not want to tear my girls from their house they call home. I felt such remorse for several years, and to be honest, I sometimes still feel guilty. I have to constantly tell myself that we are all better off this way and that I deserve to be treated better. No one wants to break up his or her family, even if there is a good reason to do so. I cried for several nights. Hearing my baby girl cry that she missed her daddy was heartbreaking. Having my oldest give me attitude because she was in a new home, which happened to be an apartment, was heartbreaking. No more house with a trampoline and a pool to have friends over. Carly did not want to have friends over if we lived in an apartment. This made me feel like shit. I was busting my ass to provide for us, and the decision was hard, but one that was mandatory. Leaving was an adjustment for everyone. Carly was very close with Alex since he was around far more than her own father, whom she only saw once a week from birth until the age of fourteen. So it was Alex who was there for her, taking her places and spending quality time with her all of those years. I sometimes think the move was the hardest on Carly, especially since she struggled for a few years afterward. Even to the point where she was self-harming. Alexa was too young to really know what was going on. Alexa was only two and a half when I left her father. A few years after the move, she had no memory of her father and me ever living together. Sometimes, when I mention a camping trip or some other event from the past, she seems very surprised that we actually used to live together. She actually asked me one time, "Wait, you and my daddy used to live together?" To which I replied, "Yes, silly." And her little eyebrows were raised and her nose scrunched up as she said, "That is just crazy." It actually brought tears to my eyes. I am not sure if this is a good thing she does not remember us as a family or a bad thing; at the very least, it was sad for sure. She thinks growing up in separate houses is normal, and it should not be, but at the same time, she didn't have to witness any arguments or any negative behaviors that some children do witness between their parents. I needed to set a good example for my girls and let them know it is not OK to be disrespected. I wouldn't want my girls to stay in a relationship like the one I was in, so why should I stay? Of course, no matter what, I feel guilty and probably always will.

 I never asked for any of this to happen. All I can do is make the best of the situation; my focus is always making sure my girls are taken care of in the best possible way. I am thankful that we can at least co-parent. We attend school functions together, and we trick-or-treat together. All other holidays are on a rotating schedule. My number one priority is always my girls, so even if I have negative relationships with their fathers, I need to remain civil. It is very important to me to let my children know that no matter what happens between their fathers and me, we both love them dearly, and they are the number-one priority. They need to know they can be themselves around either parent. It is very sickening to see parents manipulate children during a divorce or separation, and I have always vowed to never do such a thing. Therefore, no matter what I am feeling toward their fathers, I will always do my best to co-parent.

CHAPTER 6

LOSS

I have lost a few loved ones throughout my life so far. Some were harder than others; all were very sad. There is no way to prepare for the loss of a loved one; whether it is expected or unexpected, it still shatters hearts. So many mixed emotions of grief, pain, sorrow, emptiness, and many tears that follow. You would think that the more you deal with death, the easier it gets, but that is not true at all. In my case, it became harder and harder; of course, it depends on your relationship with the deceased, but no matter what, it is never easy.

My very first experience with death was when I was nineteen. My grandma passed away. I was not close with her, but I still had some memories of visiting her with my mom, and it was still very sad, especially to see my mom so heartbroken. It was also the very first corpse I had seen, so it is something I will never forget. Her face was ice cold and smelled like foundation and blush. Her cheeks were rosy and her lips red. I wondered why she had so much makeup on, and what was weird was that my mom made us pose with her. Why were my sisters and I crying beside this cold, dead body, taking a picture? It certainly was not a time I wanted to remember.

My second loss was my Papa, with whom I was very close, and I thought this was the worst day of my life at the time. I was twenty-six years old, and I will never forget this experience either. As I mentioned before, even if death is expected, it is still extremely difficult. My Papa was not the healthiest person. He was a diabetic and had emphysema, chronic obstructive pulmonary disease (COPD), and who knows what else. Not to mention he did not take care of himself; he was an alcoholic who smoked a pack a day, even when he was on an oxygen tank. However, I loved him. I loved to irritate him and make him yell at me. I was his "Scorch."

He lived in Chaumont, New York, and I spent several summers with him as a little girl. When I was older, I drove him around. I took care of him; I cooked for him and took him to many of his doctors' appointments. I loved running through the hospital halls with him in his wheelchair. I can still hear him screaming, "Slow down, Jenny, you damn fool."

The last few years of his life, I spent a lot of time with him, bringing him to most of his doctors' appointments. He developed an infection in his foot, which spread because he was diabetic, and he ended up having to have part of his foot amputated. It was disgusting. I can still see the picture of the giant hole in his foot filled with a thick greenish-black mucus. He was hospitalized, and I would visit at least four days a week. I have come to hate hospitals because of this experience, and I refuse to go to the hospital where he passed away because I feel they neglected him. He was only showered, eating, and in good spirits when one particular nurse was working. Some days, I would ask if he had eaten, and they replied no. But really, they would just set the tray in his room and walk away. How was he going to feed himself if he was high on pain meds, so weak and fragile? Why was he only bathed and smiling on days Shirley worked? It is because she clearly loved her job and actually cared for her patients. Needless to say, my Papa's health declined over the next few months. Between pneumonia and COPD complications, his organs began to shut down and he passed away. I received a phone call when I was at work. My mom said he only had a few hours to live, and everyone must get to the hospital as soon as they can to say their goodbyes. I felt sick to my stomach as I drove all the way to the hospital. My head was spinning, so many memories flashed through my head. The ride there was pretty much a blur. I was the last person in my family to arrive.

I walked in the room filled with my family standing in his room at his bedside. I lay next to him and cried so hard. I took his hand, and he squeezed it gently, and he passed away within minutes of my arrival. Everyone says he waited for me. They said they kept telling him, "Jenny's on her way." I cried so hard. This could not be happening to me. Whom will I take care of, who will make me laugh, and whom can I annoy? Whom will I spend my time with? Come back, Papa. I need you. I lay there for what seems like hours after his death, in utter disbelief. When I finally left, I took what few belongings were left behind; a pack of *Pall Mall* cigarettes, a pillowcase, and his hospital wrist band.

I took his death so hard because I was so close to him, yet I learned so much evil about him after he passed away. It is funny how everyone has a different perception of someone. The papa I knew was funny, caring, and fun to be around. He would not intentionally hurt anyone. His wish was to be cremated and then for everyone to spread his ashes in Cherry Island, New York, which is in the Thousand Islands. He wanted us to celebrate his life instead of mourn his death, so that is what we did.

The entire family rented a cottage, and we went on a boat; we drank some Busch beer, and we tossed his ashes on the island. It was an emotional day for most. However, it ended in a family feud, which might be expected after a long, emotional day mixed with drinking booze, right? We had a huge bonfire, and everyone was mourning my Papa's death, some of us telling funny stories and reminiscing, laughing at the good times we all shared. Then my dad made a comment. As he tossed the container of the remainder of ashes to the ground, he said, "He deserved to die. He was a piece of shit father and husband."

All hell broke loose. My cousins and uncles were all rolling around on the ground fighting. My uncle punched a hole in the wall of the cottage, which we had to pay for. My cousin gave his own brother a black eye. My poor nana was screaming for everyone to stop while sobbing uncontrollably. It was a mess, a sad mess.

When all this was happening, I had no idea what my dad meant. I was heartbroken over the loss of my Papa. Nana had said, "That is true, Glen, but this is not the time." At the same time, she said, "He always took everything out on Glen. Whenever he had a bad day, Glen got the worst of it out of all of the children."

What did she mean? The truth is that he was a raging alcoholic, very abusive toward all of his children and his wife. My nana used to try and protect each of her kids from the abuse of my papa. She would warn them when to hide. He spent most of his money on booze and most of his time in the bars while my nana worked at a hospital trying to make ends meet for the five children she had to raise on her own. He was very abusive to my nana and the kids, both physically and mentally. He brought his children into bars, and when they were sixteen, he brought the boys to a prostitute for their birthday. I've heard stories of him beating the shit out of my father and smashing his head into walls. What the fuck? Who was this man? Not the one I spent my time with, that is for sure. I have never seen this side of him, but I was disgusted to learn so much about him after his death.

Another day I will never forget is November 16, 2012, the day I lost my cousin David unexpectedly. His brother Chuck called me, sobbing, "David's dead; he's gone." I immediately got the chills. What happened? How?

David was kicked out of a Buffalo Bills home game held at the Ralph Wilson Stadium in Buffalo, New York, for "disorderly conduct," which he attended on November 15, 2012, with his brother and one other friend. He should have been held in contempt if he was drunk; instead they let him go. They claim he drowned near the stadium and suffered from hypothermia. He was found in a shallow creek called Slopes Creek, which is in the opposite direction from which he was supposed to be heading. David did not want his brother and friend to leave the game, so he told the boys he would walk to the bar up the road and they could pick him up afterward. They agreed—except when the time came, David was nowhere to be found, and his phone was going directly to voicemail.

The death of David was plastered all over the news because it happened at the Ralph Wilson football stadium. There was news media at my aunt and uncle's doorstep and at the funeral. It was honestly disgusting. I personally hate the media; my family was mourning an unexpected death, and how dare they try to attack the family with questions when we had so many unanswered questions ourselves? Anyone from New York knows that Bills fans are crazy. Come on, they are known as the "Bills Mafia." David was a Miami Dolphins fan, and according to the newspapers, he was being harassed for wearing his Miami gear at the game. This game alone had 94 ejections, 55 traffic tickets, 28 arrests, and 2 deaths and "quadruple the average number of ambulance requests for the sick and injured". My question is this: Is a football game worth all of that? I just couldn't be losing David. I was in shock for a long time, and I had nightmares for months. I stayed up late several nights, reading all of the articles that were published and the nasty comments football fans would write stating that he deserved this, that he was careless, that he shouldn't have worn his Miami gear to the stadium, he shouldn't have been drinking. It made me sick. I eventually had to stop googling his name and reading all of these articles and comments. Nothing was going to bring him back, and I was driving myself crazy. It was just so hard to not have answers. He was so young, funny, and talented. We were close. We had family picnics and get-togethers often; we camped and hiked and laughed together. I watched him and his band play a few at the Penny Arcade. He was definitely the cousin I looked forward to seeing the most on holidays because we would always laugh our asses off. I couldn't wait to arrive at his house every Christmas Eve for as long as I can remember; I would see him in his garage, greeting everyone who walked through their home with a hug, a kiss, and a great big smile. Nothing will ever be the same; nothing has ever been the same. Christmas has sucked without David! The family rarely gets together anymore for Christmas, or any holiday for that matter.

I have never believed that his death was an accident, especially after seeing him in his casket. I remember staring at him, noticing the bruises on his knuckles; I thought, *Was this an accident, or did he go down fighting? Why was he kicked out? Is it because he was rooting for the opposing team and these die-hard Bills fans are crazy? Why was he in the opposite direction of where he was heading? How come the Bills stadium would not release certain information pertaining to David? Did someone toss him over that fence?* Maybe my thoughts were triggered by the headlines and news articles. They sure know how to twist things or make an article appear more "interesting" by the headline. All I know is I've had several nightmares about David, and I hope one day the family gets real answers. I know my aunt and uncle were going to file a lawsuit originally, but that became more expensive and time consuming than planned, and in reality, all they really wanted was to have their son back, which wasn't going to happen. Needless to say, the lawsuit was never filed.

Below are just some of the many headlines that made the paper for several weeks after his death:

"Bad Day in Buffalo: Two Mysterious Deaths in the Shadow of One NFL Game"

(This is interesting because they write "Two Mysterious Deaths." So what really happened? Is it ironic that both people who died were Miami fans—one found in a ravine, one hit by a car crossing the road? The only thing that would make their deaths "mysterious" is if it was actually intentional. Was David tossed over the gate into the ravine? There was no sign of entry near the fence, according to police. Did the driver of the car intentionally hit this other young man? After all, the driver was a Buffalo Bills fan and the pedestrian was a Miami

Dolphins fan. If both deaths were ruled accidental, then what makes these deaths mysterious? Nothing. Nothing at all. The media sucks.)

"Family Identifies Man Found Dead after Bills Game"

"Father Left Looking for Answers after Son's Death"

"Wrongful Death or Bloody Murder?" Interestingly, this article points out that "the customary incident report that should be on file with Bills security regarding Gerken's eviction was either never made at all, or hastily destroyed, just in case."[1] I do recall reading comments on this from previous workers of the Ralph Stadium, stating that the stadium is supposed to document these evictions. *Where they are, and why don't we know which entrance he was forced to leave from? If he was drunk, then why would they let him leave in the first place?* David told his brother he didn't even know why he was being ejected from the game. To this day, there are so many unanswered questions related to this incident. I wish we had answers so we could get closure because it makes it so much harder to deal with. Although, what I want most, I simply cannot have, and that is to have my cousin back in my life.

I wanted to point out these headlines because everyone's perception of what happened is based off so much of what the media presents. There was no foul play, and many families did not receive answers as to what happened that night, so it makes everything that much harder to deal with. But not only that, the neglect of so much that went on that night. So many unnecessary injuries. People were violently attacked and seriously injured; some lost their lives. What has happened to this country, and why is all of this behavior and insubordination considered

---

[1] http://www.crimemagazine.com/wrongful-death-or-bloody-murder

normal for an event like this? It sounds like war, not an all-American football game. These are people's lives.

Two years after losing David, I lost my nana. As I mentioned earlier, Christmas Eve was no longer the same without David. His family stopped hosting Christmas Eve, and I cannot say I blame them. They hosted the first year, which was only one month after his death, which was very strong of them. I am not sure how they did it. I cannot say I would do the same. I truly cannot imagine losing one of my girls. Hopefully, I will never have to experience such a horrific event.

David's death slowly split the family apart, and Nana's death destroyed it even more. There are rarely any families that get together anymore, and when there are, they are not the same. Half the time, I force myself to go just so I can see my cousins. I cannot stand most of the adults, for I am bitter and angry over the way everyone acted the day my Nana passed. When I do go, I just want to numb myself with narcotics or booze.

CHAPTER 7

NANA

I can still hear my Nana's voice in my head loud and clear: "Honey, I'm not feeling well. I'll see you tomorrow. I love you."

Those were her very last words to me.

I was supposed to go visit her on April 17, 2014. I was planning to take her to lunch. I had an exam for one of my college courses, and I was heading to her house right after the exam. But before I was done with the exam, I received a phone call from my mom, telling me my nana had passed away. I dropped the phone and cried so hard, and then I drove to her house because everyone was meeting there. The next few hours, maybe even days, were a blur.

I remember arriving at her apartment, and several people were already there. My mom was there, with my aunts and a few cousins. My nana was sitting in an upward position on her couch with a blanket over the top of her. She lived alone. My cousin Jonathon, who had been staying the weekend with her, had placed the blanket on top of her in the middle of the night because "she felt cold." He was nine years old, and he was the only one with her when she passed away. This was much unexpected, and thankfully, it was a peaceful death. Lord knows, the woman put up with enough heartache and bullshit while she was alive. Everyone was given the chance to say their goodbyes to her before she was removed from her apartment, so people stood in a line and took turns going over to her on the couch and saying goodbye. I just remember seeing her cold, beautiful face and her bluish-purple feet sticking out from the bottom of the blanket. When it was my turn to say my goodbyes, I slowly walked toward the couch and then fell to my knees crying; I could not go near her. I could not even say goodbye.

I thought to myself this cannot be happening. I could hear her voice in my head all of the things she had said to me over the last year, especially this last week before she passed away. I had called my nana almost daily. She was my rock. I could not be losing her. I needed her.

Before she found out I was pregnant, she would say, "Have another baby before I die." This played in my head repeatedly as tears rolled down my face faster than a waterfall. You cannot die, Nana, you have not met my sweet baby girl.

"Honey, I'm not feeling well. I'll see you tomorrow. I love you." Over and over, I thought, *Why didn't I just make sure she was OK?* Jonathon said he was making her some food and that she had not been feeling well. *Why didn't anyone check on her?* She was home alone with a nine-year-old to care for her. *How does someone just suddenly pass away in their sleep? Who poisoned her?* My mind was going crazy. I just could not believe what was happening. Unbelievably, the day only got worse.

Nana had five children: two daughters (Roxanne and Elizabeth) and three sons (Glen, who is my father, Michael, and Richard). My dad arrived right before the ambulance was going to remove her. He was the last one of her children to arrive because he had been out on another crack binge. He was actually supposed to meet her for lunch the prior day, but he never showed, so now he can live with the guilt of that for the rest of his life. He can just add it to the list with the rest of the shit he should feel guilty for. I know my father has felt guilty for how he treated his mother due to his addiction. After she passed he tried to stay sober for her, but it is inevitable that this is the time his addiction only proceeded to get worse. As far as I am concerned, none of nana's children showed her the love and respect she deserved.

I sat on the floor and watched everyone turn into vultures. I could hear their greedy voices in my head as I sat on her kitchen floor in a daze as tears rolled down my face. I was numb; their voices faded in and out: "I want the knife set," "I want the couch," "I'm taking the bed." I wanted to stab the person who claimed the knife set. Simply because it was so impersonal. All of it was so impersonal. How can you sit here and claim her property like it is a goddamn auction when she has been removed from the home for only a few short hours? She was not even buried in the ground yet. You want to know what I wanted. I wanted my *nana*. That is it! I could care less about anything in that house, no matter what the monetary value was. I did not know who these people were, and from that day on, I will never view any of them the same. These vultures even cleaned the fridge out. The place was empty within hours. I was in absolute shock and disgust as everyone loaded their cars with their new possessions. You would have thought movers were hired to clean the place out.

These people were supposed to be my family, her children. They did not even seem to be mourning her death the way I felt they should. They should all be crying and feeling guilty for not visiting her as often as they should have. They should not want to live; I mean, that is how I felt at the moment. How will I survive without my nana? Then again, who are these people anyway? How does such a strong, beautiful, humble woman who came from nothing—yet who appreciated every little thing and dealt such a shit life—have such careless kids?

All my nana ever wanted was for the family to be close. She would always ask me to plan family picnics. It was joyful for her to be around everyone. She just wanted their time, and in the end, they could not even give that to her.

I wonder if she felt it was her time to go. Some of the things she was saying portrayed her outlook on how she felt about each of her children. The week before she passed, these are some things she had said to me:

"Richard lives a stone's throw away and can't even come to visit." "I give him my food stamps. Do you think he can cook me a Zweigle's hotdog?" (I had no idea she did that for him. I knew he lived close, and she was always so concerned about Richard because he has heart issues and struggles financially. He was her firstborn, and she always babied him. Why wouldn't he visit when he lived so close, and she did so much?)

"Roxanne is a pill-popping liar, and I know she stole from me. She's always too busy to take me grocery shopping." (Someone stole money out of my nana's freezer one summer. Roxanne was the only one with a key to Nana's place. I honestly always assumed it was Roxanne or my dad. However, Nana said Dad did not know about the money or have access to her house, so it made sense that it was Roxanne.) She is the only one who knew exactly where the money was.

"Michael and Molly were just around the corner the other night having dinner with Cousin Mark, and they can't even stop to say hi. Michael has not visited since I moved in." (She had moved in over a year ago. I thought, *Wow, what a piece of shit*. Once my Nana and I both moved from Naples, I saw her way less, but I still talked daily and made an effort to go see her.)

These are all very sad statements. How could her own kids not know she was so lonely? Why would they not make more of an effort to call or visit? Life is short. Do not wait until it is too late to have relationships with loved ones. Let the people you love the most know that they are loved, and make time for them. Make time for them while they are still alive. Otherwise, you will regret it when it is too late.

Nana was lonely and tired. Plain and simple. She had a long, hard life. She came from Italy and grew up very poor, which is part of the reason she was always overstocked with food in her spare food pantry. If she were alive I'd ask her more about her childhood; so I could elaborate more on her struggles; and why she came to the United States. I do know that she was not treated right by her parents and that she was raised poor. My father told me that her parents used to make her cook steaks for her brothers, and she wasn't even allowed to have any. Isn't that terrible? I am sure mistreatment from a young age had a lasting impact on her. She married an abusive alcoholic (my Papa), and she dealt with the abuse from him for many years. Yet, she was the type of person who would give people the shirt off her back and expect nothing in return. So to sit here and watch all her children, my so-called family, take all of her belongings like it was no big deal was absolutely devastating to me.

Not to mention no one even cared enough to put a headstone at her gravesite. It went several months without one. Then one day I mentioned it to my dad. I came up with one thousand dollars, and he came up with the rest of the money (about four thousand). The total was supposed to be split in five. His siblings were supposed to pay their share. The only one who paid in full was Michael. Richard never made one attempt to make one single payment, and Roxanne and Elizabeth made payments until their share was paid for, which took about six months. It absolutely disgusted me. It's like they disrespected her while she was alive and dead.

The death of my nana has been one of the hardest things I have had to deal with in my life. After she passed, I did not want to have a baby shower. What was the point if the one person who I cherished the most could not be there? Or what was the point if I didn't even want to be pregnant in the first place? I also no longer wanted to attend or host family picnics. I was done with this bullshit. I decided I had no family. I know the holidays are always the hardest for anyone who is missing someone they have lost. The holidays that are the worst for me are Easter and Mother's Day. I was with my nana every Easter and every Mother's Day for as long as I can remember. I will never forget her and I will always remember her beauty and her strength. She is the one who has taught me to be grateful and to appreciate the little things in life no matter how hard you have it, to always give to others and help others who are less fortunate because someone always has it worse. She is my hero.

I sat at her gravesite on the fifth anniversary of her death. I wrote her a letter as the tears poured down my face, and slowly dried from the warm sun.

Nana,

    Here I sit by your grave. Today is five years since you've been gone. Five long years since I have seen your beautiful face. Whoever said time heals everything <u>lied</u>. Not a day goes by that I do not think of you. I can still hear your voice the night before you passed, and I would give anything to see you again. You were my rock. I miss our daily calls, our Friday fish fry, our Sunday breakfast, and most of all, I miss being able to pop over and see you whenever I wanted. To call you whenever I want. To share good and bad news. To hear how your day was. I have told Alexa all about you, and I wish you had the chance to meet her. She certainly is sweet. We have your Cabbage Patch doll, and we named her Betty. Alexa dresses her in yellow, and sometimes she brings her to my bedroom and tells me to snuggle her. I do. It is as if she knows when I am sad. She does these things, and it brings a smile to my face, even though my heart aches and the tears fall often.

    This year Alexa picked a yellow bathing suit because "it's Betty's favorite color." It melted my heart to hear her say that and see her light up. Last year, I brought her to your grave to plant yellow flowers, and she loved it. Today I sit here alone. I prefer to come here alone because I feel more connected to you. That might sound weird, but it is as if I am actually visiting with you when I am here alone. I can feel your presence. I placed Easter eggs that the girls painted for you alongside your grave, and Alexa picked out the cutest yellow bunny plant. It is cold out, but the sun is beaming down, so it feels nice. I just do not understand why life is so hard. Why do bad things happen to good people?

I feel like you were put through hell, yet you had the most beautiful heart and soul. You were stronger than anyone I know, and you appreciated the little things in life. You were the glue in this fucked-up family. I miss family get-togethers, but I have uncovered so much bullshit about this family, so it's really just you I miss.

Some days, I feel like I am breaking inside. I do not know how you remained so positive all these years when you were surrounded by such negativity. I, for the most part, try to do the same, but some days are harder than others. I appreciate the love, the strength, and the support you constantly provided. I am forever grateful I had such a close bond with you for thirty-two years. I swear, another thirty-two would still be too short. I need you and I miss you.

I try to focus on my girls and myself. I try so hard to stay strong (like you), and sometimes, I just become weak and cry uncontrollably. I miss you more and more each passing day. I lost a part of myself the day I lost you.

I know you are watching over us. I see small signs everywhere. Fly high, stay strong, and keep shining until we meet again.

Love always,
Your sunshine

CHAPTER 8

NOAH

Almost immediately after Alex, I dated my childhood friend Noah. Noah was my rock. He sure knew what to say or do to make me feel better, not to mention he was kind of old-fashioned, which I always admired. He did things you that you do not see happen very often, such as always making sure he opened my car door for me, or any door, for that matter. No one ever opened doors for me or helped me with things. It is the little things that made me fall for him.

Depending on whom you ask, some might think I left Alex for Noah, but that is 100 percent incorrect. People only think that because I was with Noah so quickly after separating from Alex, and I was very open about our relationship. Another reason they think that is because no one really knows why I left Alex because I didn't broadcast our business. So most people did not know that our relationship was over long before we had our sweet baby girl.

Noah came to New York around Christmastime because his childhood home had burned to the ground. He lost his uncle

Charlie in the fire, and his father and brother were badly burned; they spent months in the hospital recovering. Noah was staying with his mom and driving over an hour almost daily to care for his father and his little brother. When Noah came to New York, he reached out to me, and we began to talk on the phone daily. Eventually I agreed to meet Noah for lunch one day since I worked around the corner from the hospital. Even though we were just friends, I felt so guilty meeting him for lunch because I still lived with Alex. I actually felt sick to my stomach and was not even able to eat my lunch, even though it was great seeing him. At this point, he truly just needed a friend. I could see the pain in his eyes as he spoke about his wife not wanting him to come to New York to care for his family. He said she refused to come with him and begged him not to come. I just listened as I thought, *What a rotten person*. At this point, I did not tell him what I was going through with Alex, and he did not tell me what he was going through with his wife, Becca. The more we talked, the more we learned we were both dealing with the same sort of pain. Becca had cheated on Noah, just as Alex cheated on me. But it wasn't just that; there were many other similarities in our relationships. We were both trying to make these relationships work for all the wrong reasons, the main reason being for our kids, of course. It was nice to hear that I was not the only one experiencing this pain and guilt. That I was not the only one who stayed in a relationship for the benefit of my children. I was not the only one being emotionally abused and feeling unwanted. It was nice to finally have someone to communicate what I have been dealing with for all of these years. I started to open up about my secrets I had kept for so long, and it was a relief to let it out.

I started calling Noah every day before and after work for a few weeks, before I even moved out. Alex did find out because he printed our phone bill and threw it in my face. "Jen, you don't talk to me this much. Why are you calling this asshole so much?"

"Because he is my friend, Alex, and you made me stop talking to all of my friends, and I am not going to let you control me anymore." Of course, we argued, and he tried to say that Noah was the reason I was checked out of our relationship, but it wasn't. "Hello, Alex, you cheated on me more than once, and even if it wasn't physical, each time it was still emotional, and you were unfaithful. You haven't been here for me emotionally since I've known you. You didn't even come to my nana's funeral." I couldn't trust Alex, and what is a relationship without trust? I was struggling, and I had no one; it was time to go. Not to mention I spent the entire previous year crying myself to sleep each night because I was so unhappy, so I knew damn well Noah was not the reason, not even a little bit, for this breakup.

I hung out with Noah on the very first weekend that I moved into my own apartment. It was still innocent, and at this point, I had no idea we would fall so deeply in love. But we did, and he ended up not returning to North Carolina. It all happened too fast. I was not even ready to be in any sort of relationship so quickly, but you cannot control the timing of falling in love.

In the past, even though Noah and I would go several years without speaking, we would still always pick right up where we left off. We could always talk so easily, get advice from one another, and tell jokes. We would talk for hours at a time on the phone, and no matter what we did, we were always laughing our asses off together. I never talked with anyone for hours, the conversation just always seemed to flow so smoothly with him.

It was never romantic until this point, almost twenty years later. The thing is, looking back, I see he was always there for me when I needed him, and I was always there for him, and I never knew that he liked me all along. I was completely clueless. One day we were chatting and reminiscing about our partying days when we were teenagers. He told me of a specific night that he remembers wanting to kiss me and how he always wished he had made me his girl when we were teenagers. I just laughed as I thought, *No way*. I remembered the night he was talking about because we were at his sister's house, and Noah and I were in the bathroom talking. I was upset that Scott called me "Jessica" by accident, I was pissed. Noah was just trying to make light of the situation, trying to make me laugh and just have a good time. He said the only reason he never made a move is because we were all friends and he did not want to overstep any boundaries, even if he thought Scott did not deserve me. Looking back, I can see he truly cared for me by all of the nice things he did over the years that I had never noticed, such as always thinking of me on important dates like Valentine's Day or my birthday. I remember when Scott and I first broke up, Noah sent me twelve long-stemmed roses on Valentine's Day and an Eminem CD because he knew I wouldn't be getting anything on Valentine's Day and he did not want me to be sad. At the time I thought nothing of this; I just assumed he was being a caring friend, as he always was. I saved those roses in my freezer for about ten years. I am not even sure why I saved them. I never saved any other flowers I had received in my entire life. Noah was married and living in North Carolina. He was hardly allowed to talk to me, but he did always find a way to stay in touch. He would send me postcards once in a while. I remember one particular postcard he sent. It had a very large woman lying on the beach, and on the card, he wrote, "This made me think of you, ha-ha." I laughed when I received it and thought, *What a jerk!* I kept that damn postcard on my wall above my treadmill for years and used it for motivation, even though he was joking. He had no idea that I saved the card or the flowers for so long, until I revealed it to him over ten years later, when he revealed his lifelong crush on me. Even though we were so far away for so many years, Noah would contact me every single time he was in New York, whether he had my phone number or not. He searched me out on Facebook, AIM, LinkedIn—it did not matter. He always found a way to contact me, and I was always happy he did. It did not even matter if I was in a relationship; I would just introduce him to my current boyfriend. No matter what, we made it a point to hang out before he had to leave town again. We would usually hike a waterfall or drink some beers down a dirt road or go mudding on his grandpa's property. No matter what, we were laughing the entire time. I never had so much fun with someone in my life. We just always got each other.

One year while I was dating Alex (about a year before we split), Noah sent me three very beautiful tiger lily plants at work. I gave them all away to my coworkers, and I still told Alex about it. I felt guilty, even though I did nothing wrong. Tiger lilies were my absolute favorite flower. No one had *ever* gotten them for me. At the time, I thought it was inappropriate because Noah was married to Becca, and I was with Alex. Noah said it was no big deal and just wanted me to feel special on my birthday. Well, it did make me feel special. I dated guys long term, and no one ever thought to buy me my favorite flowers, and now my childhood friend had gotten me plants so I can always have my favorite flower. How sweet! Too bad I could not keep them without feeling guilty. I knew I would not be happy if someone did something so thoughtful for Alex. So that night, I smiled, thinking of the flowers, but I was also saddened by the fact that my own boyfriend has never done something so sweet yet simple. It just confirmed Alex truly did not know me or what I liked.

So many things made Noah so special to me and so different from everyone else. I remember our first kiss. We were sitting in his big white truck in a parking lot near my work. He had called earlier to say he made me lunch and was going to stop by and drop it off on his way back from the hospital. He actually brought me lunch in a brown paper bag: a peanut butter and jelly sandwich and an apple. I thought that was the sweetest. So here we were, sitting in his truck, and he asked what I would do if he kissed me. I immediately got the butterflies and said, "Don't." He laughed and said his brother told him not to kiss me, either, because we would ruin our friendship. We were flirty. He pulled me closer and kissed me, and our teeth banged together as if we were teenagers who were kissing for the very first time ever. I swear, I had never felt like this with anyone.

Noah always knew how to make me feel special with the simplest things. I think that is what made me fall so hard. He paid attention to me, knew what I liked, made me feel beautiful and loved as no one ever had. There were simple things like braiding my hair, making me laugh, doing crafts with me, taking pictures with me; he would actually pull over if he saw a barn he knew I would want to take a picture of. No one ever did those things for me. It was truly all of those small gestures that meant so much to me because it truly showed he cared. Noah looked at my daughter as if she were his own, which melted my heart. I could see the love for us in his eyes. The way he played with her or watched her play—you could truly see he cared for her. We fell in love so fast and so hard, I truly considered him my soul mate. I still do consider him my soul mate, whether we are together or not. I could go on and on about all of the sweet things he did in just the short time we were together. Not to mention the sex was great. It was more than just sex, we made love every time. We were passionate. We were so in love; it was like we were high school sweethearts, always kissing and groping one another, sneaking off to have sex in random places. It was fun. I felt alive and young again. Imagine having a relationship with your best friend. He was my lover and my friend; it was beautiful. I'll never forget the feeling.

Our plan was for him to gain custody of his children and move them to New York. We would build our house together, and we would get married and live happily ever after. Sounds too good to be true—and it was.

It was not as easy as it sounded. Noah was going through a nasty divorce, and his wife was using the kids against him. Since Noah was now living in New York, he was not able to see his children, so he offered to pay Becca five hundred dollars to drive the kids to New York and let them spend time with him. The visit did not last long though. Once Becca realized she couldn't beg him to come back home and be with her, she took the kids and left town. I remember the night Noah and I were getting ready to make dinner plans, and Becca called and said she was in New York. So of course, he left my house and went right to his mom's to meet her and the kids. He was beyond excited to see the kids. He couldn't believe she actually drove to New York as promised. Just a few hours after Noah left my house, I was getting messages from Becca stating that Noah was trying to kiss her and that he was going to North Carolina to be with his family. I knew it was a lie. I immediately texted him and called him several times, but he did not respond for over an hour. In that hour, Becca and I shared some nasty text messages to each other. She called me a whore and home-wrecker, and I told her what a piece of shit she was for doing this to Noah and the kids. Using the kids as a weapon—how evil. Once Noah finally answered the phone, I was screaming at him. He calmed me down, and I could hear Becca screaming in the background. He told me that they took the kids to the park and his phone was in the truck the entire time, and he had no idea Becca was texting me. So he started yelling at her, and she took the kids and left. He came back to my house hours later, but I felt horrible. He showed me pictures of his kids at the playground, and his smile was so big as he talked about the kids and how great it was to see them. He apologized about Becca, but I could see the pain he was going through from missing his kids. I cannot imagine being without mine.

Noah remained in New York for an entire year after this happened. When things were good between us, they were amazing, but when they were not good, they were terrifying. Over time, it only got worse. The pain of missing his kids was taking a toll on him. He drank, and the more he drank, the bigger our problems became. He had always been a drinker, and I am sure it was a problem before this but now he was out of control.

CHAPTER 9

SUBPOENA

I often wonder why it takes me so much pain before I finally realize I deserve better. I always want to see the good in people, and the thing is, I knew what kind of person Noah is and could be, and I was hanging onto that. However, the abuse I put up with was not OK, and it only got worse as the months went on. Do you know how hard it is to give up on the one person you ever wanted to marry? Hell, the only one you even discussed marriage with seriously? The one you called your best friend and lover—your one and only soul mate? It is hard, and it is absolutely heartbreaking. What makes it even harder is when everyone around you hates the fact that the two of you are even together (including my oldest daughter). I did not care who liked him and who did not. I knew I loved him with all of my heart, and so did my youngest daughter, and I know that he loved us all unconditionally. But drugs and alcohol ruin people.

The person whom I loved so deeply, the one who made me feel the happiest in my entire life, is also the one who made me feel the absolute worst. He made me feel crazy. He was manipulative and possessive, and I did not know who this person was when he was drinking.

Once again, I saw red flags in the very beginning, but I chose to ignore them. I pacified his behavior by making excuses for him. I guess one of the first signs was when he began to try to hide the fact that he was drinking. He knew I was sick of the drinking. I made that clear very quickly. He started being sneaky about how much or when he was drinking. He would pour beer into a travel coffee mug, or he would try to "sober" up before coming home, which I later found out meant doing cocaine. Yes, that was his fucked-up thought process. He told me he would drink all day at work, and then right before coming home, he would snort a line of cocaine to "sober" up. He said it would make him sound awake and energetic instead of drunk and slurring his words.

One night, my youngest and I were downstairs watching TV, and Noah was feeling down about missing his kids so he said he was going to write in his journal upstairs. Hours later, I saw him in the kitchen pouring a glass of whiskey from an almost empty bottle. I got up and asked him what he was doing, and he slowly turned around, eyes glossed over, and said, "Drinking. Do you have a fucking problem?" That tone and that response meant he was already wasted. He never spoke to me that way when he was sober. Obviously, I had a problem. It was a Tuesday night, and he was hiding in the bedroom, drinking an entire bottle of whiskey. So we argued for a bit, and he ended up leaving. I watched him stumble to his work truck, and he put the car in drive and hit the gas instead of reverse; he almost came through my kitchen window. I was so angry. Angry that he was drinking, angry that he was yelling at me in front of my daughter, and angry he was driving his work truck completely wasted, without a care in the world. He could have killed himself or someone else. Thankfully, he returned hours later, only because he was too inebriated to find his way to his mom's house. He stumbled to bed and passed out with a mouth full of Copenhagen, which ended up staining my brand-new mattress. He woke up in the middle of the night and pissed in the corner of my bedroom, all over the floor. He made a mess of the entire house, spilling food everywhere and being completely careless and disrespectful.

We argued that night, which was pointless because he does not remember. We argued even more the next morning. Do you want to know how many times I heard, "It's no big deal"? Everything to Noah was always "no big deal." He justified every negative behavior; he blamed others for his actions. It was pointless to argue so much. I bitched about my mattress; he said, "I'll buy you a new one." I'd bitch about the messes he made; he said, "I'll clean it up." I'd bitch about him driving; he said, "So what? I came back." He always had a response, and he was never taking responsibility for his actions. These were typical reactions for a narcissist, which I truly believe he is. He definitely has several of the characteristics.

I broke up with Noah a few times due to his behavior and the way he treated me, but he always made me feel guilty, or even worse, like his behavior was my fault. He would beg, cry, and promise to change, but he never would. Each time I took him back, something worse would happen.

He left me stranded at work more than once. He stole my car, and I had to have him arrested. I had just started my new job at News Media, and he stole my damn car. I had no way to get to work. I had to call in, and I actually told my boss my car was stolen. Obviously, I did not tell her I knew who stole it. That would have been humiliating, and it was bad enough that I had to say my car was stolen. I was livid over the fact that I even had to call in to my job. I never call in unless one of my children is sick or in the hospital. This was devastating to me, and of course, it was "no big deal" to him. He made me feel like I was an asshole for calling the cops on him. I left him several voice mails stating if he did not bring my car home, I would be calling to report it stolen. He never returned my call. I had to call his family members and friends and so many people I did not know just to try and locate him. I was a wreck. I had my first anxiety attack ever. I could not breathe. I was going through so many emotions at once. I would be angry then worried. I was crying and pacing, and I could not eat, sleep, or even think straight.

The police finally located him over twenty-four hours later; he was passed out on the floor at his sister's ex-husband's house in the middle of nowhere. I had him arrested. He called several times, and he asked me to visit him in jail. I had never visited anyone in jail. I was so nervous and anxious on my way to the jail; I felt sick to my stomach. I was not allowed to bring anything inside the jail, so I left everything in my car. I slowly walked into the county jail and it seemed like everyone there knew what to do except for me. I was a lost puppy. I did not know the procedure. My voice cracked when I spoke to the officers, and I was shaky.

After checking in, I was directed to sign in and sit in a waiting room until it was time. Once it was time, a couple officers came out and loudly went over the rules: no kissing, no hugging, and no cell phones. The list went on and on, and I just remember staring straight ahead wondering how I ended up there. We walked down a cold, dark cement hallway and into a room, which had about twenty inmates on one side and some barstools on the other side, separated by Plexiglas. I felt so sick, and I started crying as soon as I saw Noah standing there in his navy-blue scrubs provided by the county jail, with his unshaven face and his dark eyes. He looked awful. I did not think he belonged there with all of those other criminals. He wasn't a criminal, he was a drunk idiot. I just wanted to hold him and tell him everything will be Ok.

I felt horrible immediately after my visit. I researched what I had to do to bail him out, and within four hours, he was back home. I bought him coffee, we went to the lake, and then we went to our first AA meeting together. I supported him for months with these meetings. I actually liked going to the meetings. I liked listening to people's stories; they were real and raw, and you could see the pain in their eyes as they each told stories of how they lost everything or how they ruined great relationships with family, friends, or lovers. I could really relate to them in one way or another. I have been dealing with addicts my entire life. I knew what it felt like to constantly be let down. The meetings helped me to understand addiction a little more. They helped me to understand what these people were going through.

The meetings were short lived. We went once a week for a few months. Noah was too far gone, and I was sick of being abused mentally and emotionally. Noah never hit me, but he had come close, and he had held me down and punched whatever happened to be above me in that particular moment. So eventually, I broke it off for good, and he decided to go back to North Carolina.

Less than one week later, he was arrested on rape charges against his wife. My very first thought was that he was innocent. I knew Becca was crazy, and I knew she had a history of false accusations against him to get him arrested whenever things were not going her way. I also know this. Within the first few days of Noah being in North Carolina, Becca was harassing me again. I was on FaceTime Noah one day, and I received text messages from Becca telling me that I was a home-wrecking whore and to stay away from her husband. She went on and on about how he was with her kissing on her as she was messaging me. Had I not been on the phone with Noah, I would have believed her. I mean, given everything I have gone through in previous relationships, it would seem accurate.

Days later, I received a call from the jail in North Carolina. The operator slowly said the words: "You have a collect call from an inmate named Noah Smith at the Lincolnton County Jail. Press one to accept this call and two to ignore this call; press three if you would like to block all calls from this caller." I remember Noah telling me that Becca set him up and had him arrested. He said he should be out of jail by Monday because it was a Friday when he had been arrested. He said everything would be sorted out, and the charges would be dropped. I asked him, "Noah, what did you do?" He said, "Nothing; the bitch set me up." Then he explained what had happened, and I believed him.

He said that she invited him over and then had him arrested for breaking and entering and that she was claiming he raped her. Immediately, I thought this was a lie; he was definitely set up. I believed Noah because this was normal for them. Becca was always having Noah arrested. In the past, she would make false claims, and then the police would have to arrest him, and once Monday came, he was free to go and was proven innocent. He always went back for his kids, he grew up without his father, and always swore he would never abandon children. I also believed him because it was only a few days prior that she was harassing me and telling me lies about him being there. Noah told me, "She's just mad because I told her we were getting back together." I asked a million questions. Was he with her? Did they do anything together? This woman said she would do whatever she could to ruin us, and she certainly did.

It did not matter what questions I asked Noah because it did not take the pain away that I was feeling. It was one thing to hear Noah explain what had happened that night, but it was a completely different feeling reading about the arrests in the paper. Imagine reading these words in the paper: "Rape (second degree), sexual offense (second degree)," alongside a mugshot of Noah with bloodshot eyes and a deep cut above his left eye. (Apparently, the officer, who was dating Becca at the time, shoved Noah's head into the ground.) I had no idea what these charges even meant. I was googling what a second-degree charge means and whether it meant he actually sexually assaulted her. I cried and I puked. I felt like I was kicked in the stomach once again.

Noah spent five months in jail, and then he was bonded out. Once he was bonded out, he came to New York. This case was going to go to trial and I was a key witness. Some days, I'd think about going to trial and getting on the stand to defend him and make Becca look like the liar that she was, and others I'd have such anxiety. I had never been subpoenaed before, and to have to testify on a rape case to defend my childhood best friend and lover was absurd to me. Regardless, now that I had to testify, I had to keep communication open with Noah.

CHAPTER 10

EMPATH

Dating Noah made me realize that I was dating someone who had the same exact characteristics as my father (and not the good ones). I always said I would never date anyone like my father; I do not know how my mother put up with him for so many years. Yet here I was, dating a raging alcoholic and caring for him endlessly. Supporting him in all ways possible. I wanted Noah to be the best version of himself, and I was determined to help make this happen. Just like I was always helping my dad, thinking if I loved him and supported him, even when no one else did, that maybe someday it would be enough to make him want to sober up, and not be a loser drug addict anymore. That is the problem though; I always want to help fix people, and I can't. People have to want to better themselves. Some say I am an empath. If someone is in pain or struggling, I always want to help, even if it means putting their needs before my own. I am currently working on putting my own needs before others.

Even though I quickly realized Noah was never going to change unless he truly wanted to change, I kept trying. I knew deep down it had to be his choice, and he had to want the help. My love and support would not make him sober, just like my dad will most likely never change. Both of these men have lost years of relationships with their children and grandchildren and many other loved ones. They have both destroyed relationships, lied, stolen, cheated. They have both totaled vehicles due to driving under the influence of either drugs or alcohol. Yet none of this was enough to sober them up.

I want you to know that I didn't just "give up" on Noah, or my father, for that matter. I went through hell in a short period of time, and all of the drunken experiences brought up a lot of emotions that I had not dealt with from my past, such as my father's addiction.

There are a few drunken nights that I experienced with Noah that I will never forget, just as there are several life events that I will never forget that I have experienced with my father's addiction, some nights where I was scared for my life.

Let's talk about one of the days Noah left me stranded at work. It was Black Friday, so I could never forget the date. The office closed earlier, so I called Noah to come pick me up. He said he was on his way, and he showed up four hours later. So for four hours, I was outside pacing the parking lot with my laptop bag. I kept calling Noah; sometimes he would answer and others he wouldn't. Each time he did answer, he would say he was on his way. I would scream because he kept saying that and then clearly was not there to pick me up. After a few phone calls, I realized he was drunk, and once I called him out on this, he stopped answering my phone calls until he was about five minutes away. I was on the phone with him when he pulled into the parking lot, eyes bloodshot and glazed over, slurring his words. I noticed a beer can in the cup holder, and I picked it up and threw it at him. I said, "You're drinking and driving my car, Noah?"

"No," he replied. And that is when I picked up the beer and threw it at him, screaming, "Then what the fuck is this?" As soon as he said, "Where was that?" I knew he was blackout drunk, and everything I said or did would be pointless. I made him get in the passenger's seat, and I told him to call someone to pick him up from my house because I did not want him staying with me that night. He called a few people, but no one would come to pick him up.

Noah knew that I was pissed off. He kept trying to kiss me once we got home. He wanted to have sex, and I did not want to have sex. He kept saying, "Let's make love, baby; don't be so mad." I was mad, though, and who the hell wants some drunk breathing heavily all over them? Not me! He wouldn't let me be though; he kept trying to take my clothes off, kissing on me aggressively. Noah hated to just "fuck" me. It was usually a turnoff to him if I said, "Just fuck me doggy style." He would roll over and say that is not what he wanted. He always wanted both of us to be "in the moment." I got so frustrated that he wouldn't leave me alone, so I turned to him and said, "Fuck me like your whores," and he did. I was shocked and devastated at the same time. I thought by saying this he would leave me alone. This made me hate him at this moment. Who the fuck was this man? How could he be so gentle and loving one minute and so aggressive the next?

After he fucked me, I continued to scream about the fact that he was an alcoholic who would never change. I started to pack up his shit from the closet. I was ripping clothes from hangers and shoving them in boxes and bags. I told him I was fed up with his reckless behavior and could no longer tolerate it. He threw me on the bed, pinned me beneath him, and told me to stop it. He said he wasn't going anywhere and I couldn't keep breaking up with him because it was breaking his heart. I laughed and said, "What the fuck do you think this is doing to me?" I kicked him off me and grabbed my phone, which he quickly grabbed from my hand and smashed to pieces, throwing it to the ground. Who was this monster I loved so deeply?

I kicked Noah out, which didn't last long; he was always back in forth between my house and his mom's. One night, he called me up and begged me to come visit him. He said he was staying with his sister and he was lonely. I asked him if he was drinking, and he said he wasn't. So after hours of him begging me to come see him, I finally caved. I drove over an hour in the middle of nowhere to go see him. I pulled into his sister's long driveway. It was pitch black; there was one light on in the house, and the rest of the house was dark. I saw Noah standing near his truck. I walked up to him and he gave me several hugs and kisses and then asked me to go for a ride with him. It felt good to be in his arms once again. It always did. I just wanted sober Noah so badly. As soon as I got in the truck, I could see an eighteen-pack of Coors Light in the back seat. As he backed out of the driveway, he reached back and asked if I wanted one. I said sure. He didn't have one at this point. Apparently, he didn't need one though. Noah started saying how everything was bullshit and that he just wanted to come home with me. He started rambling and getting all emotional, so I realized, once again, he had been drinking.

Don't ask me why, but of course I started yelling. I was pissed off that he lied to me again. I never learned to not yell when he is wasted though. Number one, it just pissed him off more, and number two, he had no recollection of what I am saying, so why was I getting so worked up? It was absolutely pointless. Yet there I sat, saying, "You lied; you said you were sober. Take me back to your sister's." He wouldn't though; he started speeding down the road as I screamed for him to stop driving recklessly before he killed us or, even worse, some other innocent drivers. My yelling just made him drive faster, though, and he was so dumb, he was making comments like "I am a better driver when I am drunk" and "I am in control; don't worry." Yeah right, Noah! You were not in control. I was so scared, I texted Hannah to tell her that I was in the middle of the woods with Noah and to call the cops if she did not hear from me that night. Obviously this worried her, and she started asking where I was, but I had no clue where I was. I couldn't even tell her what town I was in.

He drove up some hill into the middle of the woods a half hour away from his sister's house. He kept hitting the steering wheel, screaming at me. Each time he would hit the steering wheel, I would try not to flinch. I never wanted Noah to know when I was scared because I always told him I wasn't. I would push him and scream right back. In these moments, I wasn't sure who was crazier, and I hated it.

Four months later, it was Saint Patrick's Day, and we decided to have fun. I wanted to drink, and of course, this wasn't a good idea for Noah the alcoholic. But I was sick of not drinking around him because it didn't matter whether I drank or not; he would still drink, in front of me or behind my back. If he wanted a drink, he was going to have one. Bottom line. So we went out to dinner, and it was fun. There was an Irish band playing. We drank a few green beers, ate some corned beef, and laughed. It is always fun in the beginning. After a few hours and a few beers, I wanted to go because I knew if Noah kept drinking it wouldn't end well—and I was right.

We left the bar, and we went home. I fell asleep on the couch, and I woke up to Noah cooking and being loud and obnoxious on the phone, drinking beers all by himself. I sat up quickly and started screaming. Noah would not shut up about Hannah, and it was pissing me off. A few months prior to this night, Noah had driven his company work truck completely wasted, and Hannah had called his place of employment to report him. I didn't care that she did this. I knew he shouldn't have driven, and I thought maybe this would help him realize he needs to sober up. It didn't though. He just threw it in my face and constantly brought it up. This was just Noah's way of justifying everything. He was always blaming someone else. Noah started calling Hannah names, and I screamed back, defending her. I told him to leave. I was so sick of this shit. I was starting to hate him because I didn't know this person standing in front of me. When I told Noah to get out and never come back, he pinned me to the couch and held my hands down with his knees. He sat on me, screaming as loud as he could, punching the couch right above my head. I was waiting for his fist to slip and hit me. I tried to stay as still as possible so that he wouldn't hit me. The entire time, he was screaming, "You're mine, you're mine, you're mine."

Something inside me snapped. I kicked him off me, and he flew to the ground. "I am not yours, you piece of shit. *Get out!*" Noah decided to go start his car, and when he went outside, I locked the door so he couldn't get back into the house. I was shaking at this point. I thought he eventually had left, until I heard a noise on my back porch, I peeked through the blinds and saw him standing there looking past me, with that evil glossed-over look in his eyes that he got once he was to a certain point of intoxication. This right here was the look I hated and feared because I did not know the person standing in front of me.

CHAPTER 11

TRIAL

Noah ended up spending four months in jail, for the rape accusations, and then he was bonded out by his mother. This meant he was free to do what he wanted and just had to show up for court dates. Over the next several months, Noah would fly to New York and spend time with me, a weekend here or there. I had to have surgery in April of 2019, and no one was around to help me. My mom stayed with me my first night home. I was not supposed to drive for ten days, and I was driving the very next day. Alex wouldn't keep Alexa. He dropped her off with me the day I was home from surgery. So Noah flew to New York to help me take care of Alexa and assist with daily activities that I should not have been doing in the first place. This was the man I fell in love with in the first place, the one who tenderly cared for me. He was helping cook and clean, playing with Alexa, braiding my hair, massaging my back, making me rest even when I wanted to help out because I was going stir crazy. He dropped everything in North Carolina to come to New York and take care of me. He ran his own HVAC business. He could have easily been making money, and instead, he was spending money to come care for me. No one has ever done that. I had family in the same town I lived in who did not even help me or call to see if I needed help. It was moments like this that meant the most to me. These are the moments that made me hope for the best and hope he would no longer be an alcoholic.

But even in these seemingly perfect moments, there was so much emotion between the two of us that I couldn't make it work. I have never cried so much for anyone in my entire life. Noah didn't drink one drop of alcohol when he came to visit. It was his trips back home where he would get completely inebriated and call me, leaving messages like "I hope you die," "You're a whore," and "Where are you?" He just couldn't handle that I wouldn't commit after all he put me through. I don't know how many times Noah said the words, "You are mine; you will always be mine," both in person and over the phone. He truly believed I was his. I am not an object. I belong to *no one*. I always said I wasn't scared of Noah, and I wasn't, but I was scared of this monster he became when he was drunk. It definitely meant something to me that he was showing he cared for me when no one else was around, but I was definitely to a point where I was no longer in love with him. I was starting to feel mixed emotions. I was on an emotional roller coaster, and I couldn't handle it.

You would think if someone is out on bond for rape charges that they would sober up, but he didn't. He was a lying drunk up until his last day in public. He even totaled his work van and got ticketed for a DWI.

One night while drunk, Noah started making threats and talking stupid, so I called the cops on him—even though he was in North Carolina and I was in New York—all because I was afraid of the unknown. He had called me up to tell me he was going out to get wasted and beat people up for fun. I could tell he was already wasted. He was slurring his words and talking about not wanting to live anymore. He also made the comment that he could put an end to the "rape trial" with two dollars. I thought about what he was saying and then realized he was referring to a bullet. You bet your ass, I called his lawyer to tell him. His lawyer did not seem to care, so I called the North Carolina police. I did not want to call the police on the love of my life, but I was not about to sit home and say nothing because the truth is, I had no idea what he was capable of. I didn't know this person anymore. I would have felt awful if he acted upon his words and I didn't notify anyone. The next few weeks, I walked around my house with a knife in my hand in case Noah showed up unexpectedly. I didn't know what he was capable of. I wasn't sure if he would be angry that I called the police on him while he was out on bond. I knew it would not look good for his trial, but he needed to take responsibility for his actions, which is something he does not do often.

Noah did call me immediately, and he wasn't happy at all. Of course he screamed at me and called me names, telling me I was ruining his life and I should have never called the police because he was just talking stupid. He said he would never shoot anyone. What Noah didn't understand was that I didn't know who he was. Sober Noah wouldn't even say these things, but drunk Noah just might act upon these statements. He was constantly blaming me and never looking at things from my point of view. Drunk or sober, it is *not* OK to say you're going to go on a shooting rampage.

I started having anxiety attacks and breaking out in hives, the closer it came to trial. I would call my doctor and ask for medication to help control these attacks. She prescribed me Klonopin, first in a small dose of a .50-milligram tablet, which later increased to 1.5 milligrams of an orally disintegrating tablet. Klonopin was originally formulated to help people with epilepsy manage seizure attacks. The drug has a powerful, calming effect, so it is also used to treat panic attacks, which was my reasoning for taking the pills.

Not long after my phone call to North Carolina, Noah was back in New York for his sister's wedding. The same day I was walking around my house with a knife in hand was the same day I drove an hour away to meet Noah in the middle of the woods. He looked horrible. I felt sick to my stomach. He could see the hives all over my arms and neck, my puffed eyes now raw from crying. He held me, kissed me on my forehead, told me how sorry he was, and then made love to me. Even though I was sick to my stomach, I felt more at ease once I left. I cannot make sense of it, but I always felt better if I knew Noah was OK. I felt more at ease if he knew my whereabouts and I knew his. I felt safer, for some reason. My thought process was that if I updated him and stayed in touch with him, he wouldn't have a reason to want to get wasted and hunt me down. At the time, I just wanted him to go to his sister's wedding and for me to go to a concert with friends and not be completely scared the entire night. It sounds completely insane. I feel dumb writing about some of this stuff, but the truth is, this behavior on both ends is normal. It is common for alcoholics to have narcissistic traits and psychologically abuse their loved ones. He was constantly making his needs and desires seem superior, and I was too blind to see through so much abuse. Even when I did try to talk myself into not dealing with this behavior anymore, I'd always find ways to justify his behavior. I felt powerless.

Needless to say, the closer it came to trial the sicker and more emotionally unstable I became. Noah was arrested and put back in jail just weeks before the trial. This threw a wrench in our original plan. Noah was supposed to pick me up from the airport and drive me around. I was supposed to stay at his uncle's house with him. Apparently, the phone call I made months earlier finally caught up to him, and because of the threats he made, they wanted him in jail until trial so that he was not a flight risk. Of course, this, too, was my fault. If I didn't call the police, he wouldn't be in jail, right? This was thrown in my face several times, but hello! Take responsibility for your own actions, Noah. I still had every intention of going to North Carolina to defend him, even though he was blaming me for everything, including the rape charges. Apparently, it was my fault because if I wasn't talking to another man (while we were not together), then he would not have gone running to Becca in the first place.

In the end, I did not make it to the trial. I know; go ahead and judge me. Those who are close to Noah judged me and talked shit about me not flying down for trial to defend my so-called soul mate, but where were they? I wasn't the only witness, yet none of us showed up. His mom was supposed to fly down, and there were two more potential witnesses right in North Carolina: Noah's roommate and his cousin Arnold. His mom said she had anxiety for far car rides and plane rides, and I am not sure what happened to the other two. Apparently, his mom and I were the key witnesses, and we failed to appear, so that is what mattered most. I truly planned to go until the very last minute, when it all became so overwhelming. I purchased a plane ticket, and it ended up being fraudulent, so I was going to drive. *How could a plane ticket be fraudulent?* I was so distraught at this time in my life with everything going on, I just googled plane tickets, instead of going to an actual site. I clicked on a "cheap flight's" link. I was sent an email confirmation, which included an image of my plane ticket. When I looked up the departure and arrival dates on the actual airline website; there was no such flight listed. I tried calling the company I purchased the ticket from; I was unable to reach them via phone or email. I immediately googled the company I purchased the plane ticket from and that is where I read several reviews, stating this was a scam. I decided I was going to rent a car and drive to North Carolina, which is about a twelve-hour drive. I was supposed to do this by myself and stay in a town with people I don't know. I was also supposed to leave my daughters in New York, which was giving me anxiety. I have never been away from my youngest for more than a few days, and now I had to leave my children for a week—not to mention I started having crazy thoughts about Becca trying to have me arrested on bogus charges. I was supposed to be states away from my own family, not knowing where Becca would be or if she would try to have me arrested on some bogus charge. The laws were different in North Carolina. I could be thrown in jail if she made a claim I was harassing her, and that worried me. Everything about the trial worried me. I began having anxiety attacks all over again. I called my doctor and was put on medications to assist with these attacks and calm me down. I was hyperventilating, I was short tempered, and I was angry and emotional. I was not eating or sleeping. I honestly felt like I was losing my mind. All of this was new to me. I didn't know what was happening; all I knew was that

I hated feeling this way and just wanted this trial behind me so I could cut off contact with Noah completely. I was emotionally exhausted from all of this.

A few days before the trial, Noah called me from jail yelling at me, telling me everything was my fault and that I shouldn't bother coming. I was trying to explain to him how sick this was making me, and he was not being understanding at all. Instead, he told me I was selfish and that I could control these attacks. I was so angry that he didn't understand where I was coming from and that he was blaming me all over again. Screw you, Noah; you are in jail for your own actions, and I cannot control panic attacks and hives. Actually you know what? I can control them. I can control them by avoiding you, Noah. You are the cause of my excessive worrying, lack of sleep, and emotional breakdowns.

CHAPTER 12

FLING

When Noah first moved back to North Carolina, I decided that I needed to have a rebound, someone to help me get over Noah. I was losing my soul mate; I was emotionally unstable. I needed something to free my mind from all of this. I knew it was going to be a long time before I could move on from Noah, if ever. I just wanted a distraction from this emotional roller coaster I had been on.

    I started talking to an old friend named Blake. Blake would send me random pictures of sunsets or barns through Instagram and Facebook Messenger once in a while, even before I was separated from Noah. Noah knew of this because I was completely honest with him about every little thing; he would get pissed off, but I just blew it off because he was possessive. I thought he was overreacting when he would say things like, "If he is sending you pictures because he knows you like them that means he likes you." Of course, I'd tell him he was crazy. I have learned that I really am naive when it comes to shit like this. Most likely, Noah was right, but at the time, I just figured it was because he was controlling, which he definitely was at times.

When Noah moved back to North Carolina and Blake was still sending me messages, I thought to myself Blake would be the perfect rebound; he is a male whore. Well, that is what I thought anyway. It didn't help that people like Mac would fill my head on what a womanizer Blake was, or the fact that I knew a few girls he had been through in the past. Little did I know that this so-called fling would last for almost two years (one year and eight months, to be exact), off and on, of course—and I'd say more off than on.

Just weeks after Noah moved, Blake asked me to hang out, so I drove to his house, which was about forty-five minutes away from my house. We went out to a cute little country bar, which was fun. We laughed, listened to music, and drank beers, so I ended up staying at his house. We did not hook up. We made out and passed out. The next morning, I drove home, and then the following weekend, he asked me to hang out again. I am pretty sure this is when we hooked up. We may have met up for a hike in between. We hiked almost every single time we hung out, which is one thing I loved about our time together. We would hike and do things we both enjoyed. We would laugh, and we would drink beers and just be stupid together. The problem is, we never communicated well from the very beginning. I did make it known that I recently had ended a relationship, which meant I was an emotional mess.

One night, just weeks after Noah was gone, I went to Blake's house for a bonfire. His cousin and his cousin's girlfriend were there, and I knew I needed to be numb. The girlfriend was making comments like, "He must like you since you've been around more than once." Wow! Perfect, right? This confirmed he is a male whore, and I could just hook up and move on. So that night, I drank a shit ton of beers, and I took a Percocet to numb myself. I have never just hooked up with someone, and even though I knew Blake and we had hung out a few times, I also knew I was out of my comfort zone and that I definitely wasn't ready to move on. At the same time I really wanted to have sex, and I really hoped that hooking up with Blake would help me get over Noah quicker. Blake was attractive, and he was funny as hell, so why not? Well, let me tell you this—it does not work that way! Numbing yourself and having a rebound does not erase the pain of a previous relationship. The problem here was I really enjoyed hanging out with Blake, even though my mind was not always in the moment and my heart was not ready. I genuinely enjoyed our time together, and I loved that our time together distracted me from Noah.

My birthday was just two months after when Blake and I first started hanging out. Blake surprised me with such thoughtful birthday gifts when I totally wasn't expecting anything. I figured we were just hanging out. He didn't have to get me anything, but clearly he put some thought into it, which melted my heart. I thought, *Hmm, maybe he is not the person everyone portrays him as. He is actually sweet, caring, and funny.*

After only a few months of hanging out, Blake told me he loved me one night (which I never heard him say). I must have passed out, although I remember the night because I actually wasn't drinking. Shocking, I know! Anyway, the problem here is that he never told me that he even said it until months after telling me. So one night, he asked if I remembered what he said to me, and I knew right away what it was going to be: "I love you." He told me I had three guesses. I was not ready to hear the words or say them, so I guess you could say I acted immature when he told me to guess what he said that night. I guessed dumb things such as "You like it in the butt"; clearly that was not the answer. Because I failed to guess that he told me he loved me, he refused to say it again. Who was more immature here, though? Him for not being able to be man enough to repeat it and tell me how he feels, or me for deflecting and trying to be funny about it just because I didn't want to hear it? That was the start of our miscommunication, and from there, it only got worse.

I want to be clear: I was completely honest with Blake from the beginning. I told him I was just out of a relationship and that I was taking it hard. Blake also knew that I still communicated with Noah, which he hated, and I can't say I blame him. The more Blake and I hung out, the less I'd communicate with Noah, which is what I wanted so badly: to stop the communication with Noah. Some nights, Noah would blow up my phone, calling over and over. If I didn't answer, he would leave very hurtful messages, wishing death upon me and calling me names, especially if he was wasted, which most of the time he was. Sometimes, I would even block Noah's phone number so that he wouldn't be able to get through if he did call and so I wouldn't be tempted to answer if I saw his number pop up on my phone, but I'd always end up unblocking him. I couldn't let him go. He had some sort of control over me.

It didn't help that Blake would randomly stop talking to me if he was upset over something instead of communicating with me. Whenever Blake stopped communicating, I'd always get lonely and end up calling Noah. Noah knew I was hanging out with Blake, and it would piss him off, but he would always try to be my friend, which I realize now is a huge problem as well. If you are in a serious relationship with someone and it ends, there really is no way you can remain friends—not if you truly cared for that person. It was both comforting and emotional to keep in contact with Noah. In the end I had to let him go, even as a friend.

I let Blake treat me like his puppet for almost two years. He would get mad and not talk to me for a month at a time. Then he would message me, saying that he missed me and he would say things like I am his favorite person and he has never had so much fun with anyone else in his life. I'd be missing him, so we would hang out, but it was always short-lived. Maybe we'd hang out for another month, and then *bam!* I was chopped liver again. This really had an emotional impact on me. Blake would show he cared by buying gifts and sending them to my house, or sending thoughtful messages or pictures that he knew I would enjoy. But then he would start ignoring me, not bringing me around his family, and not making time for me or really showing me that he truly cared. It tore my heart apart. He didn't want to make anything official, and I was sick of it. He would always just say, "Why do we need a title?" How about because we are adults, and it has been almost two years? If I am not important enough to be your girlfriend, then why are we hanging out, and why was he so offended when I referred to him as a fling? I was not young; casual dating was never really my thing. I wanted a relationship, and I was tired of pretending that he was just a fling. He wasn't. I cared about him a lot. Blake sent very mixed signals the entire time when it came to whether or not he wanted a relationship. In the end, he told me one drunk night again, "I love you so much." He kept asking me, "Do you love me?" while we were making love, and I'd say yes. Then he would say, "Then tell me," so I did. I love you, I love you, I love you. The next morning, we acted casual as always, and one week later, it was over for good. If he loved me, it would not have been over.

I am sure you want to know what finally ended it, right? So here goes. The night Blake told me he loved me is a night he broke into my house and showed up in my room completely unannounced.

Blake and I hadn't talked in a month or so because this was one of the times that Blake was ignoring me again. Let me explain why we weren't speaking this time. This time, we weren't speaking because he saw that I had a dating app on my phone. I had not gone on any dates. I wanted Blake, but as I mentioned before, he didn't want a relationship. Since he seemed to have made it clear that he didn't want a relationship, I downloaded the dating app and talked to a few guys, but that's it. If Blake didn't want to be in a relationship, why was he so upset that I had a dating app on my phone? How long was I supposed to be his puppet? It had already been almost two years. I was getting sick of all of the back and forth and no commitment. When Blake saw that I had the dating app, he was a child about it. He did not confront me and ask me questions or tell me how he felt. Instead, he waited until he left my house, and then he messaged me that he saw the app on my phone. I tried to explain to him how I felt and why I downloaded the app in the first place. He claimed to be hurt by this and said he wasn't talking to any other girls and hadn't been the entire time we have been together. All this did was confuse me even more. So if he wasn't with anyone and I wasn't with anyone, then what was the big deal if we were in a relationship? How could he make it so clear that he didn't want to be in a relationship and then throw a fit the second I attempted to move on?

We stopped talking for a few weeks. Then one night I had messaged Blake telling him I missed him and asked him if he missed me. I told him I just wanted him to know I was thinking of him. We sent a few texts back and forth, and I could tell he was still upset about the stupid dating app on my phone. It was late, so I said goodnight and I passed out. I woke up to him in my bed kissing me all over and hugging me, telling me he missed me loved me *so much*. I was so excited to see him and shocked at the same time. I was not expecting him to show up at my house at all, especially breaking in through my kitchen window. He is over six feet tall, and he climbed through my kitchen window and tiptoed upstairs. I never heard anything. Kind of scary, huh? Scary that I didn't hear anything. I didn't care that he broke in; I was more than happy to see him.

Blake and I ended up hanging out a few days later. We had an amazing day hiking some local waterfalls, our favorite thing to do together. After our hike, we went to a local bar, had a beer and some lunch, and then went back to my place to snuggle up and watch TV and nap together. It was New Year's Eve, and he ended up leaving. I didn't want him to leave, but I wasn't about to ask him to stay if he had plans. We had just started talking again. He said he was not feeling well but he needed to go to his cousin's house and his friend's house to at least "make an appearance" because he said he would. I didn't want to stay home, and he didn't ask me to join (which I was slightly annoyed by). Once again, I was good enough for him on his terms. So I decided to text my good friend Zeb and go out. Zeb and I went and had some drinks at my girlfriend's house. While we were drinking, everyone started telling me how blind I was, and they told me how unimportant I must be to Blake for him to be treating me so poorly this entire time. They said if I was important, he would have made more of an effort all along. All of these comments made me upset, not only because I cared for him but because deep down, I knew they were all right. I mean, part of me knew this information for a while now, but it was a slap in the face hearing it from my close friends. I was starting to feel hurt and angry, and I wanted to see if Blake would meet up so that I could have a serious talk with him. I texted Blake, "Happy New Year, Blake" at midnight and he never responded. He actually stopped responding to me an hour or so after he left my house. It took about an hour to get where he was going. Convenient, huh? So he spent the entire day with me and part of the night and then left me and ignored me once he arrived at his destination. I knew damn well he wasn't sleeping before the ball dropped if he was planning on going to two different parties on New Year's Eve. I knew something was up. I'd been down this road before.

I started feeling sick to my stomach and I decided that since Blake showed up at my house unannounced a few nights prior, I would show up at his. So I dropped Zeb off at his car and I drove an hour away to Blake's house. When I pulled into his driveway, I could see he was not home, and I panicked. My first thought he must be with someone else! Why else would he ignore my calls and text and then not be home when he claimed to have a stomachache? I felt so nauseated and sick to my stomach because it was like everything was starting to make sense. Maybe all of the times Blake stopped talking to me was because he was with someone else. I knew that no matter what the case was, whether he was with someone or not, that he wouldn't be man enough to discuss this with me. I kept trying to call him over and over, and he was not answering, so I started walking around his garage. I even tried to get into his house. I wanted to just be waiting in his bed when he finally arrived home so that he would be just as shocked as I was a few nights prior. Nothing went as planned this night. Everything was locked, and it was freezing. While I was roaming around his garage, I got this dumb idea to take a few of his belongings to use as a leverage to get him to talk to me. I took his muck boots and his tripod. Clearly, I didn't want these things, and I planned to give them back. I just knew that there was no way I was waiting for him to get home because it was freezing out, and I wasn't about to actually break into his house if no windows were unlocked. I knew I had to go home, and I was angry about that. So I loaded his big ass size twelve muck boots and this stupid tripod into my car and left his house and drove back home. Another long hour. It seemed like the longest hour of my life. I think I arrived at home around four thirty in the morning. Needless to say that my plan to take his belongings for leverage didn't work. Blake didn't want to discuss anything. Shocking, I know! I ended up driving all the way back to his house two days later to return his belongings. He was not home so I placed them on his door step and left. I sent him a text message to let him know I dropped off his belonging. He never responded. I have not talked to him since.

Stupidly, I wrote him a letter telling him how I feel, and I kind of regret that. He already knew how I felt, and I was a goddamn game the entire time. At the same time, I did want him to know that I was truly sorry for the way things started and ended. I never should have tried to move on if I was not emotionally ready. I never should have been so stupid to think that a fling would help me move on from Noah. I've learned that nothing but time helps heal a broken heart.

There was so much damage done throughout this entire relationship, if that is even if you want to call it. Neither of us were ever good at expressing our feelings; we both wanted different things at different times, yet enjoyed one another's company so much that we just kept repeating the same stupid mistakes over and over. The biggest one was *not communicating*. I never felt comfortable communicating with Blake though. Why would I? I was constantly wondering if each time would be our last time hanging out. I never knew how to act around him, and he blamed the communication issue on his stupid SAT scores. Apparently he scored "below average in communications." He even showed me the scores. But really, Blake? Is that your excuse? Grow up! You know damn well you can communicate what you want to.

Part of me wanted to leave this chapter completely out of my book, but you know what? It is a chapter in my life where I did learn so much from this relationship. I learned not to move on if you are not ready. I also learned that both sides need to communicate, no matter how hard it is. If you do not put in any effort into the relationship, then the relationship is pointless. I also learned that a fling is not my style and that if I really care about someone, I need to tell them. I learned that if I am not good enough to be someone's girlfriend, then they do not deserve me at all. It is all or nothing. I am not a yo-yo. I learned that if someone wants to be with you, they will make an effort, no matter how hard it is, and most importantly, I learned to trust *actions* and not *words*. Words are just words. People say what they think you want to hear, or they say what they want to say to get what they want from you. If someone means what they say, their actions will prove it. I also learned that if you have to question where you stand in a relationship, you're clearly standing alone. In the end, I truly cared for Blake, so this was a really hard lesson for me, but I feel it was meant to be this way. Everything happens for a reason. I allowed myself to cry and mope for two days, and then I woke up and decided I am better off. I wasn't about to waste another day being sad over someone I meant nothing to. I know I wasn't perfect for this relationship. I was emotionally damaged, but I also know I made an effort to fix things, and I did communicate my feelings to Blake on more than one occasion. Once I realized Blake didn't care, or make an effort to show he cared, I realized I was better off. Thank you, Blake.

Even though I learned so much, I was still experiencing many different emotions, which is another reason why I felt it was important to add this chapter. I was hurt. I was angry—angry at myself for allowing Blake to treat me this way for so long. Part of me blamed myself. I always felt guilty for going into the relationship with the mindset that he would just be a fling, but once I referred to him as a fling in the very beginning, he always held that against me. I thought he would get over the fact that I even made that comment, but he didn't. He used it as his excuse to keep me at an arm's length, to pull me in when he wanted me and push me away when he didn't. And I allowed this behavior when I shouldn't have.

Lesson learned: I will not be rushing into relationships when I am not emotionally available.

CHAPTER 13

FAREWELL

Noah was sentenced to a few years in prison, and there was no trial because there were no witnesses. It was all he said, she said. I have no idea what his exact sentence was or which charges he was sentenced for. I believe it is somewhere around three years. I spoke with Noah for the first few months he was in prison, but it didn't take long for me to realize he was still controlling me even, from behind bars. Noah would call my phone and have me put money on his commissary (his money), but he would have me download all of these prison apps on my phone. I'd be sending money to random inmates or their family members. I'd be calling relatives of these inmates, which made me very uncomfortable. I did not know these people, and some of them were in prison for murder, and here I am calling their family members, who now had access to my phone number. Do you know how much information you can find on a person with just their phone number? *A lot.* Therefore, this made me very uncomfortable.

Noah would yell at me and make demands for me to do these money transfers, and I had no idea what they were for. He was vague about why I needed to do these transfers. Yet he was very demanding, expecting me to just drop what I was doing and run to the nearest location that does money transfers. Not to mention, he would call me while I was working and then just expect me to drop everything for him. If I said I was at work, he would respond and say, "Go on your lunch break" or "Go after work." This became frustrating that he was making these demands and then getting upset if I was too busy. I was stressed at work. I had projects with deadlines. I also had very limited time. My schedule was planned out daily between work and my daughters and their school activities. I was still an emotional mess over everything, and I realized he still had the power to control me. He was manipulating me. He made me feel like shit for not wanting to be in a relationship with him while he was in prison. He also still blamed me for most of his actions, even though I was the *only* person who had stuck by his side this entire time. His family wasn't helping him in any way that is for sure. I wanted to be with Noah. I truly wanted to marry him and live happily ever after. But after all the bullshit, the lies, the abuse, the manipulation, I had to let go. I later found out that Noah was trying to sell drugs while in jail, and that is why I had to "hurry" to send these random strangers money whenever he would call.

I was fed up with all his phone calls, demanding me to do these transfers I was uncomfortable with. I told him I was no longer going to do them, and he flipped out, saying things like, "You are never there for me." He blamed me for him being in prison once again, and I've ignored him ever since. He said some really mean things, which were typical when he was angry, yet they were unacceptable. I gave him my all. I never cheated or lied to him. (And I am pretty sure he cheated on me.) I tried to help him sober up. I helped him get back on his feet. I allowed him to move in with me so quickly after my long-term relationship with Alex ended, even though

I wasn't ready. I allowed this because he was a friend, and I knew he needed someone. I took him shopping for clothes, brought him to interviews, and encouraged him. I created his business logo; I helped him find work and think of catchy slogans for his business. I gave so much and would have gladly given so much more—but not to be disrespected and unappreciated over and over again.

I hope prison is a life lesson for him, and I hope when he gets out, he stays sober. I hope he comes out stronger and wiser. The lesson learned for this relationship is: do not lose yourself trying to save someone else. I was an emotional mess. I tried so hard to help Noah get sober, and while doing so, I had so many breakdowns. True love does not make you sick. Learn to love yourself first. I realized that if I was not healthy for myself, then I cannot be healthy for my kids, and they are truly my number-one priority.

I actually wrote a poem called "Farewell" (for Noah).

Farewell

Slurred words and bloodshot eyes,
My love for you I now despise.
If you only knew how many nights I've cried...
I forgive and forgive; you continue to lie.
I tried so hard, kept providing support.
My patience is running short.
I'm losing myself to try to help you.
It's time to explore another avenue.
So let's part ways; I wish you well.
I love you my friend, but this is farewell.

CHAPTER 14

SUICIDAL

What finally led me to therapy? What took so long to get here? I was referred in the past by my doctor, but I had never actually gone until now (besides the very few sessions I had when I was sixteen, right after being abandoned by my parents.) That only lasted a few sessions though. The guy was weird, and I was young. I didn't want to open up to some older man who sat in a chair in a dimly lit office with his stupid notebook asking me questions about how I felt. I was just shipped off to live with relatives I hardly knew, my dad was a drug addict, I was in a new school…how do you think I felt? I was young and angry, so I refused to open up.

I spent months driving to work wishing I'd die, and now my daughter was suicidal. I was at an all-time low, struggling with this depression that I have battled my entire life. I didn't want to work. I didn't care about my appearance. I had no energy, no interest in things I generally I cared about or enjoyed doing. I was just doing the bare minimum to get through each day. But I had to get my shit together and be there for my daughter now more than ever. So I made an appointment with my primary doctor, and she referred me to see a psychiatrist so they could recommend the proper medications. She said they had more experience and could figure out which medications would help stabilize my mood and help me, and she recommended therapy.

I have been on and off anti-depressants and anxiety medications for almost twenty years now; she figured the psychiatrist could prescribe something more effective. She also recommended that I start talking to someone in order to start dealing with all of my emotions and anger. She stressed the importance of needing to be there for my girls and said if I do not get help, who would be there for them? *Valid point.* My girls are my world, so I agreed to finally speak with a therapist.

If my daughter was suicidal, she needed to speak with a therapist, and I was trying to be a good role model and let her know that it is OK to get help; it is OK to need to talk to someone and to have several different emotions. I just wanted her to know it was all OK and that the emotions she was experiencing were normal. I realized that she needed to deal with these emotions before it was too late. I did not want her to hold on to emotions for several years as I had done. I've learned that suppressing your emotions hurts your mental and physical health.

Finding out my daughter was suicidal was one of the most heart-wrenching things I have experienced in my life. I had meetings with school counselors; I was constantly worrying if I would wake up and find my daughter dead in her room. I was losing sleep. I was waking up to check on her in the middle of the night to make sure she was still breathing. I would slowly tiptoe into her room and place my hand on her back or under her nose to make sure I could feel that she was breathing. I woke her up a few times, tripping over whatever objects were scattered on her bedroom floor. I had to constantly hide razors and search her room. I remember feeling so nauseated when I found a razor blade that she had retrieved from a pencil sharpener. She took apart a pencil sharpener to cut herself. I was in disbelief. This is something I would have never thought to even do. It did not matter if I was hiding sharp objects, she always finds something to use.

I will never forget the day I noticed that both of Carly's arms were cut from her wrists up to her elbows; my stomach sank. I really should have been used to this sickening feeling, but I was not. I cannot even explain what that feeling was like. My stomach was beyond queasy. My head was spinning. My sweet baby girl wanted to end her life. Doesn't she know she is the only reason I want to live my life? (Well, her and Alexa.) Literally the only reasons I have to live for—everything I do is for them. I had a million thoughts running through my head. My main question was *why? Was* she sexually assaulted? *What was she dealing with that was so deep that she couldn't express herself?* I spent hours researching teen suicide, what to look for, and why teens self-harm. I would get the girls ready for bed and then lie awake for hours reading articles on suicide and teenage cutting. I'd read until my eyes hurt, or until I cried so much I couldn't read anymore. It was all so sad. Sometimes I'd just write poems or quotes for hours in my journal, trying to deal with all of my emotions. So many emotions that have been bottled up for so many years. Writing definitely helps, I have shared a few poems I have wrote throughout this book, each pertaining to my own life experiences. The truth is, I am still struggling, and my daughter is still self-harming. We are working with physiatrists and therapists and it is not easy. I know that I try even harder to focus on my mental health so I can be there for my girls. I do not want my daughter to hold secrets in for decades, like I did. I want her to talk to someone about her pain and struggles now. I want her to stop self-harming. I want her to live a happy and fulfilling life, as she deserves. We all deserve to be happy. We all need to work on our own mental health.

Suicidal

Angry and unsure why,
I stay locked in my room and cry.
Collecting pins and razor blades,
daydreaming of better days.
My wounds don't heal; they just get worse.
This depression and anxiety—a family curse.

Feelings

Feeling desolate, shattered, and defeated.
Will I ever feel completed?

CHAPTER 15
ADDICTS

I have been surrounded by drug addicts my entire life. I am really surprised I didn't end up at junkie myself. I am pretty sure that if I hadn't had Carly, I would have been an alcoholic, but who knows? I was young, so maybe it was just considered normal to party as much as I did before I had her. Either way, I consider her my lifesaver. However, the past few years, I took pain pills that were prescribed to me, yet I abused them. I didn't use them when I was actually in pain. I used them when I wanted to feel numb, when I didn't want to deal with my shitty life and everything I was going through. Physical pain was much more tolerable than emotional pain. In case you are wondering I did talk to my therapist about abusing the pills briefly, just to make sure I didn't have a problem. The abuse was brief, thankfully, I did not become addicted. I only took the pills I was prescribed for surgery. Besides, if I am working on myself I want to be one hundred percent honest during these therapy sessions.

Even though I have been surrounded by addicts my entire life, I will just never fully understand addiction. I just cannot imagine something so powerful that you throw your entire life down the drain. It seems silly to even want to try such drugs in the first place, knowing that they can make you powerless. Maybe that's the problem. People just think they are in control when the reality is they are not in control.

The two reasons I do not experiment with drugs and *never* will are my daughters, Carly and Alexa. I would never want to not be able to provide for them. I guess I shouldn't say *never*, considering I have done 'shrooms and I've smoked marijuana. I mean that I will never become a victim of the heroin or cocaine epidemic we are currently facing in this country. I never want my girls to go through what I have gone through or witness what I have witnessed. I have watched my dad slowly spiral out of control my entire life. It is not easy to watch the ones you love throw their life away so carelessly. Not to mention, his addiction caused paranoia in my life for decades.

I have lost several close friends due to addiction, several classmates, and a few acquaintances. All of these losses were heartbreaking to witness, especially knowing I still have so many addicts in my family, and I am just waiting for the day I get the call saying my father or another relative is dead due to an overdose. I remember one year, my father was so bad, I used to wish that he would overdose. Isn't that awful? I don't think people realize the power of addiction or the toll it takes on a loved one. Addiction is a family disease; one person's addiction destroys the *entire* family.

My father has missed a lot of family events and life experiences due to his addiction. I have made countless dinners for him for Father's Day or his birthday, where I have cooked his favorite meals and desserts and bought gifts for him, and he never shows. This was always heartbreaking, no matter how often it happened.

I would blame myself when he let me down. It was my fault I kept believing his words and not his actions. I was the fool. One year, my father didn't show up to a dinner I made, and I went looking for him. I knew the area where the crack house was, and I decided I was going to drop him off his birthday card and gift. So I drove around in the ghetto for about an hour, just a scared little white girl determined to make her father feel like shit for bailing on her once again. The problem is I was dumb for thinking he would feel like shit. All this did was hurt me even more. When I found my father, I beeped and he looked over in my direction. He then came dancing over to the car like nothing was wrong, completely forgetting it was his birthday and that we had plans. He was smiling as he leaned his head into my car and said, "What's up, sweetheart?" I told him I brought him a birthday card, and his response was, "wow, too cool!" as he danced around my car. What the fuck is cool about this, Dad? Your daughter just brought you a birthday card in the damn ghetto at a crack house. He was high out of his mind; he reeked of drugs and booze, he looked like hell, and all this did was devastate me and make me want to drink, to numb myself. This was not the reaction I was looking for. I wanted him to apologize for missing dinner. I wanted him to feel guilty for allowing his own daughter to be exposed to a crack house. I could see crack whores sitting on the porch. These women were disgusting, with their un-brushed hair; their trashy, skimpy clothes; and their lack of self-respect. These are the moments that made me determined to *never* become an addict.

"Crack Pipe" is a poem that I wrote after one of my father's car accidents. It was after this accident that I realized I needed to cut ties with my father. I realized he will most likely never change. If he hasn't yet, then what are the chances he will before one of us passes away? I'll tell you what the chances are: slim to none! Looking at my dad in a wheelchair, broken ribs and all, seeing him in pain and also seeing that he was itching to leave the hospital to get back to the streets was absolutely disgusting and heart-wrenching at the same time. I realized I was done worrying and making myself sick. I was sick of the constant disappointment. Even though he has been so rotten and done so many awful things and put my family in shitty situations, it is still so hard to cut him out of my life. He is still my father. I still love him; I just cannot maintain a father-daughter relationship with him any longer.

Crack Pipe

Up for days, smoking crack,
Lying in the ER on my back.
Several broken ribs and a totaled car.
while driving home from the bar.
The past few days are such a blur.
What happened you ask? I am unsure.
Doctors said I am lucky to be alive.
This pain I'm feeling I cannot describe.
Just get me out of here; set me free.
I need my crack pipe, so let me be.

It took me a very long time to get to this point, the point at which I need to cut ties with people, regardless of my love for them. I learned that I need to set healthy boundaries for myself and my own two daughters. I need to stop making excuses for their behavior and stop bailing them out when they are in trouble. All this is doing is enabling their poor behavior. I was letting their behavior affect my social life and my mental health. I do not know how many times my dad has called and begged for money or followed me places, including my place of employment, to beg for drug money. Usually he would lie and say he needed gas or cigarettes, but those lies got old quickly. Either way, I would always cave and give him the money—not because I wanted him to go get high, but because, at that particular moment, I wanted him out of my sight. I didn't want him at my job or at the playground around my children. I just wanted him out of my face. It was humiliating, whether people around me knew what was happening or not. I always felt like everyone knew what was going on. My dad was high off his ass. If I knew, others had to, right?

My life has always been consumed with everyone's problems. I know I am not the only one. I know there are several people in similar situations, and they all need to know that it is OK to walk away from an addict or anyone who has a negative impact on their life. Once it affects your lifestyle, once you neglect yourself, know that it is not worth it.

The addict will change when they want to. The question is: Do you want to continue to allow their behaviors to affect your mental or physical health? I know it took me decades to realize I no longer want to be a part of anyone's negative life choices, whether they are drug related or not. Life is too damn short to be anything but happy.

CHAPTER 16

EMOTIONAL NEGLECT

I never realized the impact that emotional neglect throughout my life from my parents and in my relationships would affect me as an adult. As I got older, I started having mixed emotions consisting of anger, guilt, shame, depression, diminished self-esteem, and relationship difficulties.

Being forced into unwanted physical situations at a young age made it hard to trust others, especially when you are feeling neglected by your parents, the people who are supposed to love and support you the most throughout your life. I had no one in whom I could confide. I had to keep this dirty secret bottled up for decades. I became really independent at a young age, and throughout my life, it has been (and still is) hard for me to accept help from people who actually want to help. Growing up, I knew I had no one I could truly count on, so it is really hard to allow others to be there for me as an adult. I am OK with being independent, although I am still trying to work on this. I know that in a relationship, you need to be able to count on each other. I always make it known to my significant other that I am there for them, no matter what; they can always count on me. However, I also make it known that I am independent, which sometimes comes off as "I don't need you." In my head, I don't need them. I don't need anyone. It does not mean that I do not want anyone. I am trying to work on allowing others to be there for me. I want a healthy relationship. I want to be able to count on someone, and I want them to be able to count on me. Otherwise, what is the point of the relationship?

As far as self-esteem goes, I never realized until recently that this was even an issue. I am honestly my own worst critic. I am constantly talking down to myself in order to motivate myself. Talking negatively to myself may seem motivating in the moment, but all it is really doing is limiting my ability to believe in myself, which lowers my confidence even more. This lack of self-esteem stems from childhood as well. Growing up, I have always heard negative comments about my weight. The surprising part is that these comments came from my closest relatives, the ones who are supposed to lift you up, not bring you down. I think that is why it had such a negative impact on me. When I was between the ages of fourteen and sixteen, I even struggled with bulimia.

Another thing I noticed is that when I do receive compliments, especially from the opposite sex, I do not believe them. I know; it is horrible. In the back of my mind, I am thinking, *Yeah, whatever, you tell every girl she is pretty* or *you are only saying that to be nice*. I automatically assume the guy who is complimenting me just wants something from me, when in reality, they are just being genuine. I may feel flattered for a brief second; then, instantly, I feel a sense of distrust. I love to give compliments. I know a simple compliment can go a long way and make someone feel good. So If I see something I like, I always compliment the person. It makes me happy to see their smile and know they feel good about themselves, yet I cannot accept a compliment myself.

I am constantly overthinking every situation in my life, and I hate it. I overanalyze every single thing. I sabotage potential relationships. I push people away, not because I want to, but because the second I feel neglected, my immediate response is to distance myself so I don't end up hurt. I never used to be this way. I used to trust everyone until they gave me a reason not to, and then I'd still give them chances. It was the constant letdown in my life that has shaped me to be this way. I am slowly taking the necessary steps to love myself and learn new behaviors so that I can turn negative effects of emotional neglect around. Even though I may be aware of my feelings and behaviors, it is not easy to change them.

Battling depression and anxiety is tough. Some days, I feel great; on others, I do not want to get out of bed. I force myself to get up and function like a normal human being. It is not easy, and I have felt discouraged for feeling this way for so long. I am tired of people not understanding me. No one knows what it is like. I want to be alone most of the time because I feel alone, even when I am surrounded by people, since no one understands what I go through. My mom makes comments like, "What do you have to be sad about?" or "What makes you feel anxious?" I don't know, Mom! I do not know why I feel the way I feel some days. I try hard to fight it. Some days, I just sleep for hours; some days, I just want to be numb. All I know is that I am recognizing all of these emotions. I am dealing with past trauma, and I am working on bettering myself. It will all take time, but I will get there.

EPILOGUE

Even though I may be "forever tarnished" by each of my life experiences (which is exactly what they were—life experiences!), and although they may not be great experiences, they have made me stronger. I know that I have a lot of emotions to deal with, and I will continue to deal with them through therapy. I know that it will take time. I do not believe in blaming life events on the way I react to situations. Even though these events have caused me to have a tarnished view of myself, I am recognizing the negativity and am willing to do whatever I need to become more confident in myself and my relationships. I need to have a better self-image so that my girls will have positive images.

I am working on ways to recognize my negative reactions and behaviors, learning new coping mechanisms for the pain and emotions that I feel that give me that "want to be numb feeling." I am grateful that I am able to recognize when I am acting out in anger or some other emotional state of mind.

About a month into therapy, I started having several nightmares—nightmares consisting of sexual abuse or nightmares about my father overdosing in a drug house or being murdered.

Nightmares of my grandmother's and my Cousin David's deaths. No matter what the topic of the nightmare, there is usually a common denominator. I am either being abused or neglected. When I have nightmares about the death of my loved ones, I am usually freaking out in my dream—panicking or crying, searching for help—and often, there will be other family members that appear in these dreams, but they always look so calm, and they do not seem to care about the tragedy that is occurring. Crazy how these dreams actually relate to my real-life feelings, huh? Apparently, this is normal. Even though these nightmares are causing me inner conflict and stress, talking about them is what brings light to the underlying issues I am struggling with. As I continue to talk about my feelings and deal with them through therapy, these nightmares should become more infrequent. I could probably write a book an entire book on all of my fucked-up nightmares and how they relate to what I am feeling. Instead, I just want you to realize the connection of your dreams and your realities.

If you take anything away from this book, I hope it is that you should never settle for anything less than what you deserve, regardless of how hard it may be to walk away. Always respect yourself. Never keep such dark secrets buried for so long. Never hesitate when you should act on something. Hesitation keeps you from moving forward. Deal with problems head on instead of burying them, or they will reveal themselves in ways you didn't realize were possible. Most importantly, walk your own path, learn from your experiences, and love yourself.

JENNIFER GERKEN, *FOREVER TARNISHED*

Author and poet with a Bachelors' degree in Human Resource Management; loves the outdoors; has two beautiful daughters, and lives in upstate New York.